Waterloo
Recollections

Waterloo Recollections

Rare First Hand Accounts,
Letters, Reports and Retellings
from the Campaign of 1815

edited by

Frederick Llewellyn

LEONAUR

Waterloo Recollections: Rare First Hand Accounts, Letters,
Reports and Retellings from the Campaign of 1815
edited by Frederick Llewellyn

FIRST EDITION

This is an original Leonaur book—never before in print

Published by Leonaur Ltd

ISBN: 978-1-84677-239-9 (hardcover)
ISBN: 978-1-84677-240-5 (softcover)

http://www.leonaur.com

Publisher's Note

Contents

Introduction

There is a tendency among compilers of books such as this to recycle *ad infinitum* material that is already well known, both to students of the Napoleonic era and enthusiastic readers alike. In compiling this book, my main aim has been to put before the reader a selection of reports and accounts of Waterloo that may not be wholly familiar.

Whereas I cannot claim that everything here will be totally new to you, this book does, for instance, bring together all of Captain Gronow's recollections of the Waterloo Campaign for the first time.

"Preparations for War" by Major W. E. Frye has, I believe, never been published in this form before. Frye was on furlough in Brussels as the build-up to the Waterloo Campaign began and wrote enthusiastic and copious letters to a friend, which were eventually published in an obscure travelogue. I have edited those letters with some relevance to our subject to produce the account here.

The accounts of the Gordon Highlanders and the Greys at Waterloo have been rescued from a little known book of previously unpublished Napoleonic material that has been out of print for almost a century; the journal of Jardin Aine, Napoleon's equerry is from the same source as are several other pieces here.

The final piece in this book, "Waterloo" by D. H. Parry, is a retelling of the campaign, that adopts an almost novelistic approach to offer an account that is both exciting and highly readable.

Sprinkled throughout this book are short accounts and official reports, from the perspectives of many of the nations involved, which lend truth to the old adage that there will be as many different accounts of an event as there are witnesses to it.

Frederick Llewellyn
March, 2007

Preparations for War

from the letters of
Major W. E. Frye

Preparations for War

From 1799 to 1822 W. E. Frye was a serving officer in the British army. In 1799, he took a part in the British Expedition to Holland. In 1801 he was in Egypt with Lord Abercrombie's army and received the medal for war service. He served for six years in India, during which time he visited the three presidencies and Ceylon. In 1814 he returned on furlough to Europe and was in Brussels during the Waterloo campaign. The following account of military activities in Belgium during the build-up to Waterloo, has been adapted from Frye's letters to a friend which were originally published as part of a travelogue. The closing few pages have all the immediacy of a television news report of a breaking story, complete with innaccuracies and uncertainties concerning events that have yet to be accurately documented.

Bruxelles, May 1, 1815. I had scarcely been three months in England, when the return of Napoleon from Elba, and the extraordinary dislocation of the Bourbons from the throne of France, summoned Europe again to arms.

I had reason, about six weeks before the news of this event reached London, from some conversation I had with a friend, who had just returned from a tour on the Continent, to suppose that the slightest combination against the Bour-

From *After Waterloo: Reminiscences of European Travel 1815-1819* by Major W. E Frye

bons would prove successful, from their injudicious conduct and from the temper of the people; but I never could have supposed that the return of the man of Elba would be hailed with such unparalleled and unanimous acclamation.

As I had long ago wished for an opportunity of visiting the continent of Europe, which had never before occurred to me, I eagerly embraced the offer made to me by my friend Major-General Wilson, formerly Lieut.-Governor of Ceylon, to accompany him on a military tour through the country about to be the theatre of war.

The war will no doubt commence in Belgium, and of course the Emperor Napoleon will be the assailant, for it cannot be supposed that, after the act of ban passed against him, he will remain tranquil, and not strike the first blow, which may render him master of Belgium and its resources.

We embarked at Ramsgate on the first of May for Ostend on board of a small vessel bound thither. Our fellow passengers were two officers of dragoons, several commissaries with their servants, horses, etc. After a passage of twenty-four hours, we entered the harbour of Ostend at one o'clock the following day.

The General and myself went to put up at the Tête d'Or, the only inn where we could procure beds; and we embarked early next morning at the embouchure of the canal on board of a *treckschuyt* which conveyed us in three hours to Bruges.

The landscape between Ostend and Bruges is extremely monotonous, it being a uniformly flat country; yet it is pleasing to the eye at this season of the year from the verdure of the plains, which are all appropriated to pasturage, and from the appearance of the different villages and towns, of which the eye can embrace a considerable number. There is a good road on the banks of the canal, and the troops, on their line of march, enlivened much the scene.

Bruges, formerly the grand mart and emporium of the

commerce of the East, not only for the Low Countries, but for all the North of Europe, seems, if we may judge from the state of the buildings and the stillness that prevails, to be also in a state of decline. We however had only time to visit the Hotel de Ville before General Wilson hired a carriage for the journey to Ghent. The distance is about thirty miles. We arrived at Ghent about six in the afternoon of the 4th and had some difficulty in finding room, as the different hotels were filled with officers of the allied army; but at length, after many ineffectual applications at several, we obtained admission at the Hotel de Flandre, where we took possession of a double-bedded room, the only one unoccupied. Ghent seems to be a very neat, clean and handsome city, with an air of magnificence about it. A great many French officers are also here, they seem principally to belong to the Gardes du Corps.

The next morning after breakfast we set out on our journey to Bruxelles. At one o'clock we stopped at Alost to refresh our horses and dine. At the *table d'hôte* were a number of French officers belonging to the Gardes du Corps. On entering into conversation with one of them, I found that he as well as several others of them had served under Napoleon, and had even been patronised and promoted by him; but I suppose that being the sons of the ancient *noblesse* they thought that gratitude to a *parvenu* like him was rather too plebeian a virtue. Some of them, however, with whom I conversed after dinner seemed to regret the step they had taken. "If we are successful," said they, "it can only be by means of the Allied Armies, and who knows what conditions they may impose on France? If we should be unsuccessful, we are exiled probably for life from our country."

We arrived at Bruxelles late in the evening and put up at the Hotel d'Angleterre.

This morning, the General and myself went to pay our respects to the Gran Capitano of the Holy League, and we left our cards. He is, I hear, very confident of the result of the campaign.

The reflecting people here are astonished that Napoleon does not begin the attack. The inhabitants of Belgium are in general, from all that I can hear or see, not at all pleased with the present order of things, and they much lament being severed from France and do not disguise their wish to be reunited to France nor hesitate to avow their attachment to the Emperor Napoleon.

The preparations for the grand conflict about to take place are carried on with unabating activity; the conscription is rigorously enforced and every youth capable of bearing arms is enrolled. Almost all the officers of the Belgian army and a great proportion of the soldiery have served with the French and have been participators of their laurels; one cannot therefore suppose that they are actuated by any very devouring zeal against their former commander.

This city is filled with British and Hanoverian troops. Their conduct is exemplary, nor is any complaint made against them. The Highland regiments are however the favourites of the Bruxellois, and the inhabitants give them the preference as lodgers. They are extremely well behaved (they say, when speaking of the Highlanders) and they cheerfully assist the different families on whom they are quartered in their household labour. This reflects a good deal of credit on the gallant sons of Caledonia. Their superior morality to those of the same class either in England or in Ireland must strike every observer, and must be mainly attributed to the general prevalence of education in their land. Wherever the people are enlightened there is less crime; ignorance was never yet the safeguard of virtue.

A woman who had some Highlanders quartered in her house told me in speaking of them: *"Monsieur, ce sont de si bonnes gens; ils sont doux comme des agneaux."*

"Ils n'en seront pas moins des lions an jour du combat," was my reply.

Namur, May 12, 1815. We left Brussels yesterday afternoon, and having obtained passports to visit the military posts we went to Genappe, a small village half-way between Bruxelles and Namur, where we brought to for the night at a small but comfortable inn called Le Roi d'Espagne.

Two battalions of the regiment Nassau-Usingen are quartered in Genappe. We arrived at Namur this morning at nine o'clock and put up at the Hôtel d'Arenberg.

On the road we stopped at a peasant's house to drink coffee; and we were entertained by our hostess with complaints against the Prussians, who commit, as she said, all sorts of exactions on the peasantry on whom they are quartered. Not content with exacting three meals a day, when they were only entitled to two, and for which they are bound to give their rations, they sell these, and appropriate the money to their own use; then the demand for brandy and *schnapps* is increasing. But what can be expected from an army whose leader encourages them in all their excesses?

Blucher by all accounts is a vandal and is actuated by a most vindictive spirit. The Prussians reproach the Belgians with being in the French interest; how can they expect it to be otherwise? They have prospered under French domination, and certainly the conduct of the Prussians is not calculated to inspire them with any love towards themselves.

I asked this woman why she did not complain to the officers. She answered! *"Hélas, Monsieur, c'est inutile; on donne toujours la même réponse: 'Nichts verstehn,'"* for it appears when these complaints are made the Prussian officers pretend not to understand French.

Namur is now the head-quarters of Marshal Blucher.

On the high road, about two miles and a half before we

reached Namur, we met with a party of Prussian lancers, who were returning from a foraging excursion. They were singing some warlike song or hymn, which was singularly impressive.

The Prussian cavalry seem to be composed of fine-looking young men, and I admire the genuine military simplicity of their dress. One sees in it none of those absurd ornaments and meretricious foppery which give to our cavalry officers the appearance of Astley's men.

Mons, May 14, 1815. We started yesterday morning at four o'clock from Namur. The whole road between Namur and Mons presents a fine, rich open country abounding in wheat, but not many trees. We stopped to breakfast at Fleurus, at an inn where there were some Prussian officers. One of them, a lieutenant in the 2nd West Prussian Regiment, had the kindness to conduct us to see the field of battle where the French under Jourdan defeated the Austrians in 1794. It is at a very short distance from the town; he explained the position of the two armies in a manner perfectly clear and satisfactory to us.

The Prussian officers all seem very eager for the commencement of hostilities, and their only fear is that all these mighty preparations will end in nothing; *viz.*, either that the French people, alarmed at the magnitude of the preparations against them, will compel the Emperor Napoleon to abdicate, or that the Allies will grow cool and, under the influence of Austria, bring about a negotiation which may end in a recognition of the Imperial title and dynasty. They would compound for a defeat at first, provided the war were likely to be prolonged. In the meantime, reinforcements continue to arrive daily for their army. We hear but little news of the intentions or movements of the other Allies; it being forbidden to enter into political discussions, it is difficult to ascertain the true state of affairs.

At a small village between Binch and Mons we were stopped by a sentinel at a Prussian outpost and our passports demanded. Neither the sentinel, however, nor the sergeant, nor any of the soldiers present, could read or understand French, in which language the passport was drawn up; but the sergeant told me that the officers were in a house about a quarter of a mile distant and that he would conduct me thither, but that he himself could not presume to let us pass, from not knowing the tenor of our passport.

I went accordingly with the sergeant to this house. There I found the officer commanding the piquet and several others sitting at table, carousing with beer and tobacco and nearly invisible from the clouds of smoke which pervaded the room. I explained to the officer who we were and requested him to put on the passport his *visa* in the German language, so that the non-commissioned officers at the various posts through which we might pass would be able to understand it and let us pass without hindrance.

This he did accordingly and we proceeded on our journey. We arrived here in the evening and put up at the Hôtel Royal. We found at Charleroi, Binch and here, a number of people employed in repairing and reconstructing the fortifications. Men, women and boys are all put in requisition to accelerate this object, as it is the intention of the Belgian Government to put all the frontier fortresses in the most complete state of defence.

On ascending one of the steeples this morning we had a fine view of the surrounding country and of the height of Genappe, which are close to Mons and memorable for the brilliant victory gained by Dumouriez over the Austrians in 1792. The landscape presents an undulating campaign country, gentle slopes and alternate plains covered with corn, as far as the eye can reach, and interspersed with villages and farmhouses. A battalion of Hollanders—a very fine body of men—marched into Mons yesterday evening; the rest of the garrison is composed of Belgians, chiefly conscripts.

Leuze, May 15, 1815. Yesterday morning we left Mons and proceeded to Ath to breakfast. A multitude of people were employed there also at the fortifications. The garrison of Ath is composed of Hanoverians.

There was so little remarkable to be seen at Ath that we proceeded to this place shortly after breakfast and arrived at one o'clock, it being only ten miles distance between Ath and Leuze. We took up our quarters with Major-General Adam, who commands the Light Brigade of General Sir H. Clinton's division. This brigade is quartered here and in the adjacent farmhouses. General Adam, though he has attained his rank at a very early age, is far more fitted for it than many of our older generals, some of whom (I speak from experience) have few ideas beyond the fixing of a button or lapel, or polishing a belt, and who place the whole *Ars recondita* of military discipline in pipe-clay, heel-ball and the goose step. Fortunately for this army, the Duke of Wellington has too much good sense to be a martinet and the good old times are gone by, thank God, when a soldier used to be sentenced to two or three hundred lashes for having a dirty belt or being without a *queue*.

Leuze, May 16, 1815. Yesterday morning we paid a visit to Tournay, which is distant from Leuze about ten miles, and we breakfasted at the Signe d'Or. We then proceeded to pay our respects to the Commandant General A.C. Van Diermen. The garrison consists of Belgians.

General Van Diermen. had been some time in England as a prisoner of war. He was made prisoner, I think he said, at Batavia. He received us very politely, and not only gave us permission to visit the works of the citadel, but sent a sergeant to accompany us. The new citadel is building on the site of the old one, and, like it, is to be a regular pentagon. The fortifications of the city itself are not to be reconstructed; these of the citadel, which will be very strong, rendering them superfluous. The sergeant was a native of Würtemberg and had served in the army of his own country and in that of France in most of the campaigns under Napoleon. He was a fine old veteran, and very intelligent, for he explained to us the nature of the works with great perspicuity. From the number of workmen employed in repairing the citadel, it will not be long before it is placed in a respectable state of defence. We learned that some of the Hanoverians had been deserting.

In return we met with a young French hussar who had come over to the Allies. He seemed to be an impudent sort of fellow, and said, with the utmost *sang-froid*, that the reason he deserted was that he had not been made an officer as he was promised, and he hoped that Louis XVIII would be more sensible of his merits than the Emperor Napoleon.

This morning we went to assist at a review of General Clinton's division, on a plain called *Le Paturage*, about seven miles distant from Leuze. The Light Brigade and the Hanoverian Brigades form this division. The manoeuvres were performed with tolerable precision, but they were chiefly confined to advancing in line, retiring by alternate companies covered by light infantry and change of position on one of the flanks by *échelon*. The British troops were perfect; the Hanoverians not so, they being for the most part new levies. In one of the *échelon* movements, when the line was to be formed on the left company of the left battalion, a Hanoverian battalion, instead of preserving its parallelism, was making a terrible diversion to its right, when a thundering voice from the commander of the brigade to the commandant of the battalion: *"Mein Gott, Herr Major, wo gehn Sie hin?"* roused him from his reverie; when he must have perceived, had he wheeled up into line, the fearful interval he had left between his own and the next battalion on the left.

Grammont, May 18, 1815. We left Leuze yesterday afternoon and arrived here at seven in the evening in order to be present at the cavalry review the next morning. We partook of an elegant supper given to us by our friend, Major Grant of the 18th Hussars.

The whole cavalry of the British army passed in review this morning before the Duke of Wellington, who was there with all his staff and received the salutes of all the. It was a very brilliant spectacle. The Duke de Berri was present. I think I never beheld so ignoble and disagreeable a countenance as this prince possesses. I thought to myself that he had much better have stayed away from this review; for he must be insensible to all patriotism who could take pleasure in contemplating a foreign force about to enter and ravage his own country.

General Wilson does not intend to return to Bruxelles. I shall accompany him as far as Ghent and then return to Bruxelles to await the issue of the contest.

Bruxelles, June 11, 1815. I took leave of General Wilson at Ghent on the 22nd of last month and immediately returned here, I frequently meet Prussian officers who on coming in to visit Bruxelles put up here.

We have just learned the proceedings of the *Champ de Mai* at Paris, by which it appears that Napoleon is solemnly recognized and confirmed as Emperor of the French. This intelligence sent a young Prussian officer, who sat next to me, in a transport of joy, for this makes the war certain.

The Prussians seem determined to revenge themselves for the humiliation they suffered from the French during the time they occupied their country, and I sincerely pity by anticipation the fate of the French peasants upon whom these gentlemen may chance to be quartered. Terrible will be the first shock of battle, and it may be daily expected, and dreadful will be the consequences to the poor inhabitants of the seat of war.

Cannot this war be avoided? I am not politician enough to foresee the consequences of allowing Napoleon to keep quiet and undisturbed possession of the throne of France; but the consequences of a defeat on the part of the Allies will be the loss of Belgium and the probable annihilation of the British army; certainly the dissolution of the coalition, for the minor German powers, and very likely Austria also, would be induced to make a separate peace. We can clearly see that Napoleon has not now the power he formerly possessed and that the Republican party, into whose hands he has thrown himself, seem disposed not only to remain at peace, but to shackle him in every possible manner. It is evident, too, that his last success was owing to the dislike of the people to the Bourbons from their injudicious and treacherous conduct; and the threats and impossible language held by the priests and emigrants towards the holders of property paved the way for the success of his enterprise and enabled him to achieve a triumph unparalleled in history.

On the contrary, by forcing him to go to war, should he gain the first victory, Belgium will be re-united to France, all the resources of that country brought into the scale against the Allies; Napoleon will be more popular than ever, the Republican party will be put to silence, the enthusiasm of the army will rise beyond all restraint, and, in a word, Napoleon will be himself again. The other Allies can do little without the assistance of England, and our finances are by no means in a state to bear such intolerable drains.

As to the Prussians, on minute enquiry I do not find that they were so ill-treated by the French as is generally believed, and that, except the burden of having troops quartered on them (no small annoyance, I allow), they had not much reason to complain. The quartering of the troops on them and the payment of the war contributions was the necessary consequence of the occupation of their country by an enemy.

Troops continue to arrive here daily, and now that the ceremony of the *Champ de Mai* is over, we may expect that Napoleon will repair to his army and commence operations.

Bruxelles, June 17, 1815. Napoleon arrived at Maubeuge on the 18th and the grand conflict has begun. The Prussians were attacked on the 14th and 15th at Ligny and driven from their position. They are said to have suffered immense loss and to be retreating with the utmost confusion. Our turn comes next. The thunder of the cannon was heard here distinctly the most part of yesterday and some part of our army must have been engaged. Our troops have all marched out of Bruxelles in the direction of the frontier. In the affair with the Prussians we learn that the Duke of Brunswick was killed and that Blucher narrowly escaped being made prisoner.

Bruxelles, June 18, 1815. The grand conflict has begun with us. It is now four o'clock p.m. The issue is not known. The roar of the cannon continues unabated. All is bustle, confusion and uncertainty in this city.

Cars with wounded are coming in continually. The general opinion is that our army will be compelled to retreat to Antwerp, and it is even expected that the French will be in Bruxelles tonight. All the townspeople are on the ramparts listening to the sound of the cannon. This city has been in the greatest alarm and agitation since the 16th, when a violent cannonade was heard during the afternoon.

From what I have been able to collect, the French attacked the Prussians on the 14th, and a desperate conflict took place on that day, and the whole of the 15th, when the whole of the Prussian army at Ligny, Fleurus and Charleroi was totally defeated and driven from its position; a dislocation of our troops took place early in the morning of the 16th, and our advanced guard, consisting of the Highland Brigade and two Battalions of Nassau-Usingen, fell in with the advanced guard of the French Army commanded by Marshal Ney near Quatre-Bras, and made such a gallant defence against his *corps d'armée* as to keep it in check the whole day and enable itself to fall back in good order to its present position with the rest of the army, about ten miles in front of Bruxelles. Indeed, I am informed that nothing could exceed the admirable conduct of the corps above mentioned.

Yesterday we heard no cannonade, but this afternoon it has been unceasing and still continues. All the caricatures and satires against Napoleon have disappeared from the windows and stalls. The shops are all shut, the English families flying to Antwerp; and the proclamation of the Baron de Capellen to the inhabitants, wherein he exhorts them to be tranquil and assures them that the *Bureaux* of Government have not yet quitted Bruxelles, only serves to increase the confusion and consternation. The inhabitants in general wish well to the arms of Napoleon, but they know that the retreat of the English Army must necessarily take place through their town; that our troops will perhaps endeavour to make a stand, and that the consequences will be terrible to the inhabitants, from the houses being liable to be burned or pillaged by friend or foe.

All the baggage of our Army and all the military *Bureaux* have received orders to repair and are now on their march to Antwerp, and the road thither is so covered and blocked up by wagons that the retreat of our Army will be much impeded thereby. Probably my next letter may be dated from a French prison.

Bruxelles, June 21. Judge of my astonishment and that of almost everybody in this city, at the news which was circulated here early on the morning of the 19th, and has been daily confirmed, *viz.*, that the French Army had been completely defeated and was in full flight, leaving behind it 220 pieces of cannon and all its baggage, wagons and *munitions de guerre*.

I have not been able to collect all the particulars, but you will no doubt hear enough of it, for I am sure it will be *said* or *sung* by all the partisans of the British ministry and all the Tories of the United Kingdom for months and years to come; for further details, therefore, I shall refer you to the Gazette. The following, however, you may consider as a tolerably fair *précis* of what took place.

The attack began on the 18th about ten o'clock and raged furiously along the whole line, but principally at Hougoumont, a large *Métairie* on the right of our position, which was occupied by our troops, and from which all the efforts of the enemy could not dislodge them. The slaughter was terrible in this quarter. From twelve o'clock till evening several desperate charges of cavalry and infantry were made on the rest of our line. Both sides fought with the utmost courage and obstinacy, and were prodigal of life in the extreme. But it is generally supposed that our army must have succumbed towards the evening had it not been for the arrival of Bulow's division of Prussians, followed closely by Blucher and the rest of the army, which had rallied with uncommon celerity. These moved on the right flank of the French, and decided the fortune of the day by a charge which was seconded by a general charge from the whole of the English line on the centre and left of the French.

Seeing themselves thus turned, a panic, it is said, spread among the young Guard of the French army, and a cry of *"Sauve qui peut! nous sommes trahis!"* spread like wildfire. The flight became universal; the old Guard alone remained, refused quarter and perished. The Prussian cavalry being fresh pursued the enemy all night, *l'épée dans les reins*, and it may be conceived from their previous disposition that they would not be very merciful to the vanquished. Indeed, on the 15th, it is said that the French were not very merciful to them.

The loss on both sides was very great, but it must have been prodigious on the side of the French. The whole Allied

Army is in full pursuit. Several friends and acquaintances of mine perished in this battle, *viz.*, Lieut.-General Sir T. Picton, Colonel Sir H. Ellis and Colonel Morice.

Bruxelles, June 22, 1815. This morning I went to visit the field of battle, which is a little beyond the village of Waterloo, on the plateau of Mont St Jean; but on arrival there the sight was too horrible to behold. I felt sick in the stomach and was obliged to return. The multitude of carcases, the heaps of wounded men with mangled limbs unable to move, and perishing from not having their wounds dressed or from hunger, as the Allies were, of course, obliged to take their surgeons and wagons with them, formed a spectacle I shall never forget. The wounded, both of the Allies and the French, remain in an equally deplorable state.

At Hougoumont, where there is an orchard, every tree is pierced with bullets. The barns are all burned down, and in the courtyard it is said they have been obliged to burn upwards of a thousand carcases, an awful holocaust to the War Demon.

As nothing is more distressing than the sight of human misery when we are unable to silence it, I returned as speedily as possible to Bruxelles.

Bruxelles, June 28, 1815. We have no other news from the Allied Army, except that they are moving forward with all possible celerity in the direction of Paris. You may form a guess of the slaughter and of the misery that the wounded must have suffered, and the many that must have perished from hunger and thirst, when I tell you that all the carriages in Bruxelles, even elegant private *equipages, landaulets, barouches* and *berlines*, have been put in requisition to remove the wounded men from the field of battle to the hospitals, and that they are yet far from being all brought in.

The medical practitioners of the city have been put in requisition, and are ordered to make domiciliary visits at every house (for each habitation has three or four soldiers in it) in order to dress the wounds of the patients. The Bruxellois, the women in particular, have testified the utmost humanity towards the poor sufferers. It was suggested by some humane person that they who went to see the field of battle from motives of curiosity would do well to take with them bread, wine and other refreshments to distribute among the wounded, and most people did so.

For my part I shall not go a second time.

Napoleon, it is said, narrowly escaped being taken. His carriage fell into the hands of the Allies, and was escorted in triumph into Bruxelles by a detachment of dragoons. So confident was Napoleon of success that printed proclamations were found in the carriage dated from "Our Imperial Palace at Laecken," announcing his victory and the liberation of Belgium from the insatiable coalition, and wherein he calls on the Belgians to re-unite with their old companions in arms in order to reap the fruits of their victory. This was certainly rather premature.

De Grouchy on Wavre
from a letter

De Grouchy on Wavre

Dinant, June 20th, 1815

It was not till after seven in the evening of the 18th of June that I received the letter of the Duke of Dalmatia, which directed me to march on St. Lambert, and the attack General Bulow. I fell in with the enemy as I was marching on Wavre. He was immediately driven into Wavre; and General Vandamme's corps attacked that town, and was warmly engaged. The portion of Wavre on the right of the Dyle was carried; but much difficulty was experienced in debouching on the other side. General Girard was wounded by a ball in the breast, while endeavouring to carry the mill of Bielge, in order to pass the river, but in which he did not succeed, and Lieutenant-General Aix had been killed in the attack on the town.

In this state of things, being impatient to co-operate with your majesty's army on that important day, I detached several corps to force the passage of the Dyle, and march against Bulow. The corps of Vandamme, in the mean time, maintained the attack on Wavre, and on the mill, whence the enemy showed an intention to debouch, but which I did not conceive he was capable of effecting. I arrived at Limale, passed the river, and the heights were carried by the division of Vichery and the cavalry. Night did not permit us to advance further, and I no longer heard the cannon on the side where your majesty was engaged.

I halted in this situation until day-light. Wavre and Bielge were occupied by the Prussians, who, at three in the morning of the 18th, attacked in their turn, wishing to take advantage of the difficult position in which I was, and expecting to drive me into the defile, and take the artillery which had debouched, and make me re-pass the Dyle. Their efforts were fruitless. The Prussians were repulsed, and the village of Bielge taken. The brave General Penney was killed.

General Vandamme then passed one of his divisions by Bielge, and carried with ease the heights of Wavre, and, along the whole of my line, the success was complete. I was in front of Rozierne, preparing to march on Brussels when I received the sad intelligence of the loss of the battle of Waterloo. The officer who brought it informed me, that your majesty was retreating on the Sambre, without being able to indicate any particular point on which I should direct my march. I ceased to pursue, and began my retrograde movement.

The retreating army did not think of following me. Learning that the enemy had already passed the Sambre, and was on my flank, and not being sufficiently strong to make a diversion in favour of your majesty, without compromising the army which I commanded, I marched on Namur.

At this moment, the columns in the rear were attacked. That of the left made a retrograde movement sooner than was expected, which endangered for a moment the retreat of the left; but good dispositions soon repaired every thing, and two pieces which had been taken, were recovered by the brave twentieth dragoons, who, besides, took an howitzer from the enemy.

We entered Namur without loss. The long defile which extends from this place to Dinant, in which only a single column can march, and the embarrassment arising from the numerous transports of wounded, rendered it necessary to hold for a considerable time the town, in which I had not the means of blowing up the bridge. I entrusted the defence of

Namur to General Vandamme, who, with his usual intrepidity, maintained himself there till eight in the evening; so that nothing was left behind, and I occupied Dinant.

The enemy has lost some thousands of men in the attack on Namur, where the contest was very obstinate; the troops have performed their duty in a manner worthy of praise.

(Signed) *De Grouchy*

The Battle of Ligny
an official French report

The Battle of Ligny

On the morning of the 16th, the army occupied the following position:

The left wing, commanded by the Marshal Duke of Elchingen, and consisting of the first and second corps of infantry, and the second corps of cavalry, occupied the positions of Frasné.

The right wing, commanded by Marshal Grouchy, and composed of the third and fourth corps of infantry, and the third corps of cavalry, occupied the heights in the rear of Fleurus.

The emperor's head-quarters were at Charleroi, where were the Imperial guard and the sixth corps. The left wing had orders to march upon Les Quatre Bras, and the right upon Sombref. The emperor advanced to Fleurus with his reserve.

The columns of Marshal Grouchy being in march, perceived, after having passed Fleurus, the enemy's army, commanded by Field-marshal Blucher, occupying with its left the heights of the mill of Bussy, the village of Sombref, and extending its cavalry a great way forward on the road to Namur; its right was at St. Amand, and occupied that large village in great force, having before it a ravine which formed its position.

The emperor reconnoitred the strength and the positions of the enemy, and resolved to attack immediately. It became necessary to change front, the right in advance, and pivoting upon Fleurus.

General Vandamme marched upon St. Amand, General Girard upon Ligny, and Marshal Grouchy upon Sombref. The fourth division of the second corps, commanded by General Girard, marched in reserve behind the corps of General Vandamme. The guard was drawn up on the heights of Fleurus, as well as the cuirassiers of General Milhaud.

At three in the afternoon, these dispositions were finished. The division of General Lefol, forming part of the corps of General Vandamme, was first engaged, and made itself master of St. Amand, whence it drove out the enemy at the point of the bayonet. It kept its ground during the whole of the engagement, at the burial-ground and steeple of St. Amand; but that village, which is very extensive, was the theatre of various combats during the evening; the whole corps of General Vandamme was there engaged, and the enemy fought there in considerable force.

General Girard, placed as a reserve to the corps of General Vandamme, turned the village by its right, and fought there with his accustomed valour. The respective forces were supported on both sides by about fifty pieces of cannon each.

On the right, General Girard came into action with the fourth corps, at the village of Ligny, which was taken and retaken several times.

Marshal Grouchy, on the extreme right, and General Pajol, fought at the village of Sombref. The enemy showed from eighty to ninety thousand men, and a great number of cannon.

At seven o'clock, we were masters of all the villages situated on the bank of the ravine which covered the enemy's position; but he still occupied with all his masses the heights of the mill of Bussy.

The emperor returned with his guard to the village of Ligny; General Girard directed General Pecheux to debouch with what remained of the reserve, almost all the troops having been engaged in that village.

Eight battalions of the guard debouched with fixed bayonets, and behind them four squadrons of the guards, the cuirassiers of General Delort, those of General Milhaud, and the
grenadiers of the horse-guards. The old guard attacked with
the bayonet the enemy's columns which were on the heights
of Bussy, and, in an instant, covered the field of battle with
dead. The squadron of the guard attacked and broke a square,
and the cuirassiers repulsed the enemy in all directions. At
half-past nine o'clock we had forty pieces of cannon, several
carriages, colours, and prisoners, and the enemy sought safety
in a precipitate retreat. At ten o'clock the battle was finished,
and we found ourselves masters of the field of battle.

General Lutzow, a partisan, was taken prisoner. The prisoners assured us, that Field-marshal Blucher was wounded. The
flower of the Prussian army was destroyed in this battle. Its
loss could not be less than fifteen thousand men. Our's was
three thousand killed and wounded.

On the left, Marshal Ney had marched on Les Quatre Bras
with a division which cut in pieces an English corps that was
stationed there; but, being attacked by the Prince of Orange
with twenty- five thousand men, partly English, partly Hanoverians in the pay of England, he retired upon his position at
Frasné. There a multiplicity of combats took place; the enemy
obstinately endeavoured to force it, but in vain. The Duke
of Elchingen waited for the first corps, which did not arrive
till night; he confined himself to maintain his position. In a
square attacked by the eighth regiment of cuirassiers, the colours of the sixty-ninth regiment of English infantry fell into
our hands. The Duke of Brunswick was killed. The Prince of
Orange has been wounded. We are assured that the enemy
had many persons and generals of note killed or wounded. We
estimate the loss of the English at from four to five thousand
men. On our side it was very considerable, it amounts to four
thousand two hundred killed or wounded. The combat ended

with the approach of night. Lord Wellington then evacuated Les Quatre Bras, and proceeded to Gemappe.

In the morning of the 17th, the emperor repaired to Les Quatre Bras, when he marched to attack the English army: he drove it to the entrance of the forest of Soignes with the left wing and the reserve. The right wing advanced by Sombref in pursuit of Field-marshal Blucher, who was going towards Wavre, where he appeared to wish to take a position.

At ten o'clock in the evening the English army occupied Mont St. Jean with its centre, and was in position before the forest of Soignes: it would have required three hours to attack it; we were therefore obliged to postpone it till the next day.

The head-quarters of the emperor were established at the farm of Oaillon, near Planchenoit. The rain fell in torrents. Thus, on the 16th, the left, wing, the right, and the reserve, were equally engaged, at a distance of about two leagues.

The Heroes of Hougomont
the Guards at Waterloo

by E. Bruce Lowe

The Heroes of Hougoumont

The success of the battle of Waterloo turned upon the closing of the gates of Hougoumont.

Wellington

All British and French writers agree that the chateau and farmhouse of Hougoumont formed the key to Wellington's position at Waterloo. When Lord Uxbridge asked the Duke which was the material point of his operations in case any accident should overtake him, the reply was, 'Keep Hougoumont.' Victor Hugo, describing the battlefield, writes:

> Hougoumont: this was the beginning of the obstacle, the first resistance which that great wood-cutter of Europe called Napoleon encountered at Waterloo the first knot under the blows of his axe. Behold the court, the conquest of which was one of Napoleon's dreams. This corner of earth, could he but have seized it, would perhaps have given him the world likewise.

To hold this vital point in his line of battle, Wellington chose the Coldstream Guards, under Lieutenant-Colonel Sir James Macdonell, a gigantic, broad-shouldered Highlander from Invergarry; and to these same broad shoulders and the *perfervidum ingenium Scotorum*, which at the supreme moment and crisis of the assault refused to yield, Wellington after the battle accorded the laurels of victory. When appealed

41

to, in awarding the prize of five hundred pounds bequeathed to 'the bravest soldier in the British army at Waterloo,' Wellington wrote:

> The success of the battle of Waterloo turned upon the closing of the gates of Hougoumont. These gates were closed in the most courageous manner at the nick of time by Sir James Macdonell. I cannot help thinking, therefore, that Sir James is the man to whom you should give the five hundred pounds.

Like a true Highland gentleman, Macdonell handed over the money to the stalwart sergeant who, shoulder to shoulder with this colonel of the Guards, had forced back the door on its hinges in face of overwhelming numbers of the enemy. The following details of this incident are gathered from the most reliable French and British sources.

The Coldstream Guards, who, with the 3rd or Scots Guards, formed the 2nd Brigade of General Cook's Division of Guards, arrived on the field of battle at five o'clock on the evening of the 17th June, wearied with the long march from Quatre Bras, where they had helped the Highland Brigade to win a costly victory. It was then a fine evening; but at seven o'clock, when Macdonell's men advanced to take possession of the chateau and grounds, a tremendous storm of rain, wind, lightning, and loud thunder broke over the country. Nor were they a moment too soon; for hardly had they closed the gates before a party of French cavalry approached at full speed and sought to seize the orchard. A short and sharp encounter satisfied the enemy that the attempt with their numbers was fruitless.

All that night the small garrison were kept at work by Macdonell in strengthening the buildings for defence; and in the morning they started to pierce the brick walls of the orchard and garden for loopholes, and to erect low platforms for the second firing-line which should shoot over the walls. All the gates giving access to the chateau or the farm were barricaded with flagstones, beams, broken wagons, and the like; but the great North Gate leading to the British ridge was left open to allow of free ingress for ammunition and reinforcements if necessary. This open gateway constituted a source of much danger, as by a rush the enemy might at any moment force an entrance before a sufficient number of the defenders could rally to the spot.

Early in the morning of the 18th, Wellington and his staff rode down to the spot. Muffling, the Prussian officer, and other foreigners were with them. Taking a survey of the defences, the Duke expressed himself well satisfied.

'Now Bonaparte will see how a general of Sepoys can defend a position,' he said; and was about to remount, when Muffling expressed some doubt as to the possibility of the post being held against assault. Wellington merely pointed to Macdonell, to whom he had been giving some final instructions, and remarked, 'Ah! you do not know Macdonell.'

After the battle after Napoleon had sent his brother Jerome against Hougoumont; after the divisions of Foy, Guilleminot, and Bachelu had hurled themselves against it; after nearly the entire army corps of Reille had been employed against it, and had miscarried; and Kellerman's iron hail had exhausted itself on this heroic section of wall Wellington again met Muffling near the chateau, and shouted exultingly to him, 'Well, you see, Macdonell held Hougoumont after all.'

The first French gun was fired at half-past eleven, and was the signal for a general advance of their 6th Division, under Jerome Bonaparte, which attacked the wood on the south side of the position with great impetuosity, in the face of a heavy artillery fire from Major Bull's howitzer horse battery to whom the Duke gave orders in person with the effect that the French columns were twice checked ere they entered the wood and drove off the Hanoverians and Nassauers posted there. Time after time the attack was renewed, the defenders contesting every inch of ground and making a rapid advance at the first indication of hesitancy in the attack.

Slowly and surely the French infantry pressed back the skirmishers of the Guards through the beechwood into the alley of holly and yew trees running round the north and west sides of the position. Under the belief that this hedge formed the only obstacle to a rush into the garden and or-chard, the Frenchmen, mistaking the red colour of the brick wall for the British uniform, sprang rapidly forward only to find themselves the target for a deadly fire, which burst upon them from loopholes and platforms along the garden wall. Though staggered for a time, the assailants, rendered frantic by the unexpected obstacle, and constantly reinforced from the main body, rallied, and obtaining a vast preponderance of force, swept round the flanks of the farmhouse, and, like the onward sweep of a tidal wave, carried all opposition before them.

The French had ascertained that the defenders received their supplies of ammunition and were being reinforced from time to time by way of the great North Gate. It was therefore determined to make a fierce onslaught on this portion of the line of defence. To this point, accordingly, General Bauduin, the Commander of the first Brigade of Jerome's Division, di-rected the advance of the 1st Regiment of Leger Infantry. Later, seeing Bauduin fall mortally wounded just before the gateway was reached, the colonel, Cubieres, assumed the di-rect command, and with loud shouts rode forward towards the one vulnerable spot in the armour of the defence. In or-der to beat down all opposition he ordered forward a party of *Sapeurs*, at whose head he placed a brave young officer, the Sous-Lieutenant Legros, but better known among the sol-diers as *L'enforceur*, otherwise 'the smasher,' who, though at the time an officer of Light Infantry, had served for a period with the Engineers, and was recognised by all as a brave and capable leader for the task in hand.

Seizing a hatchet, and waving his comrades to follow, Legros rushed past the blazing haystack, the dense black smoke from which filled the lane and hid from the defenders the terrible danger which now threatened their position. At this critical moment the group of Guardsmen who had been holding tenaciously to the lane leading to the gateway were compelled by the overwhelming smoke and heat produced by the burning hay, and now by the rapidly increasing pressure of their enemies, to relinquish their post. Seeing themselves about to be outflanked and their retreat cut off by a force now entering the 'friendly hollow way' from the other or east end, the Guards withdrew into the great courtyard of the farm, and hastened to close the great North Gate.

THE FORGOTTEN RANK AND FILE

This handful of Guardsmen, upon whose courage and devotion to duty must now depend the fate of Hougoumont, and, in Wellington's own words, 'the success of the battle of Waterloo': who were they? From contemporary newspapers, from short obituary notices, and from the lists of Yeomen of the Guard, Bedesmen of Westminster Abbey, Tower, and Chelsea Pensioners, and the like, it has been possible to trace a few of these brave men. How difficult the task has become is shown by the fact that Mr Dalton's *Roll-Call* published in 1890, contains the names of but a few out of the many who fought in the rank and file of the regiments of Foot Guards. Thousands are as forgotten as 'autumnal leaves that strew the brooks in Vallombrosa'.

The party now retiring slowly into the courtyard consisted of men from the light companies of the Coldstreams and of the 3rd or Scots Guards. Among them were two brothers, Graham by name, natives of the County Monaghan, also two sergeants of the Scots Guards Bryce, M'Gregor, a native of Argyleshire, who enlisted at Glasgow in 1799, and remained in the service till 1822; and Sergeant-Major Ralph Fraser, a veteran who had served with distinction in Egypt in 1801, in Hanover, at Copenhagen, and in the Peninsula, where he was twice badly wounded. Upon these men then fell the brunt of the determined attack of Cubieres' regiment, headed by Legros and his *Sapeurs*.

A fierce hand-to-hand fight now ensued. Step by step the gallant defenders were forced to give ground. Then, in order to create a diversion, Sergeant Fraser, while his comrades made for the gate, rushed forward into the thickest throng of the enemy, alone and at great personal risk, and attacked the mounted officer whom he saw urging his charger forward with the obvious intention of preventing the heavy gates from being closed. With a powerful thrust of his sergeant's halberd he pulled the officer, who was no other than Cubieres himself, from the saddle; and then, with a swiftness which utterly disconcerted the Frenchmen around him, he 'rode into the courtyard on the Frenchman's horse' before the surprised assailants had realised his daring design.

Fraser was, however, closely followed by Legros and about a hundred of the enemy, who, parrying the vigorous bayonet-thrusts of the defenders, threw their combined strength upon the partially closed gate; and, mid the crash of falling timbers and the rattle of crumbling masonry, the great North Gate of Hougoumont was captured.

Only for a moment did victory rest with the Frenchmen. Attracted by the loud shouts of *'Vive l'Empereur!'* and the counter-cries for help from the hard-pressed defenders of the gate, Macdonell, calling the three officers near him to follow, made for the courtyard. The sight which met his gaze was sufficient to stagger even the bravest heart.

Already a hundred Frenchmen had entered the gateway, and some had penetrated as far as the wicket-gate of the inner yard by which he and his party must pass from the garden to reach the North Gate. Here a dozen Frenchmen of the 1st Leger Regiment had been surrounded by a number of Hanoverian infantrymen, who had been driven into the garden from the orchard by the overwhelming numbers of the enemy. In a few moments the fight here was over, and the intruders hunted down; but not before the Frenchmen had the satisfaction of seeing a young Hanoverian lieutenant, Wilder by name, pursued by another party of Frenchmen towards the farmhouse, and, at the moment when he grasped the handle of the door, cut down by a ferocious *Sapeur*, who hewed off his hand with an axe.

On entering the courtyard, Macdonell saw that the Guardsmen there were defending themselves at the entrance to the cow house and stables which ran eastwards from the gate, and that several of their number were lying wounded at the doorway. Among these latter was one of the brothers Graham of the Coldstreams. From the windows of the parlour, 'from behind the walls, from the summits of the garrets, from the depths of the cellars, through all the air- holes, through every crack in the stones, the Guards, now in ambush, were firing upon the French in the yard. At the chateau, the defenders, besieged on the staircase and massed on the upper steps, had cut off the lower steps.'

However, it was not to be. Macdonell, as we have said, was a man of giant stature and breadth of frame; and when he rushed like an infuriated lion upon the Frenchmen around the gate they scattered before him. With him were a handful of young officers. They were, like Colonel Macdonell, all officers of the Second Battalion of the Coldstreams.

Captain Harry Wyndham was a son of the third Earl of

Egremont, and had already seen eight general engagements in the Peninsular war, although on the day of the battle of Waterloo he was not yet twenty-five years old. Besides earning immortal fame by the heroic deed which we are now about to relate, Wyndham is remembered by an incident which occurred immediately after the battle as darkness was falling upon the field. Pressing on in the general pursuit of the French, he saw one of the Imperial carriages attempting to escape, and soon ascertained that the occupant was none other than Napoleon's brother Jerome against whose columns he had been fighting all day. Quick as thought he opened the carriage-door, only to catch a glimpse of Jerome as he leapt out by the other door and disappeared in the darkness.

Sergeant John Graham

Following Wyndham into the courtyard came Ensigns Gooch (afterwards Colonel) and Hervey; and as they approached the small tower and well in the centre of the farmyard they were joined by Sergeant John Graham of the light company of their regiment, who, as already described, had, with his now wounded brother and Sergeants Fraser and MacGregor, been holding the enemy in check and preventing them from setting the stables and barn near the great North Gate on fire. As this small party approached the gate there appeared before them, at the further end of the narrow way, a strong reinforcement of French infantry pouring in from both flanks. The British officers became at once roused to frenzy by the thought of the dire calamity which must befall the whole army if they should fail. With Hougoumont taken, Napoleon would entrench himself in the key to the British position, enfilading the right wing and opening the highway by the Nivelles road direct to Brussels.

The little party of officers no sooner burst in fury upon the Frenchmen near the gate than they turned tail and broke up into several parties, some taking refuge in the open cart-shed adjoining the gate, and others making for the barn, where many of the British wounded were lying, and through which there was a direct road to the south or French side of the position. The remainder stood their ground, awaiting the arrival of the reinforcements now in sight.

In less time than it takes to relate, Macdonell and Sergeant Graham placed their broad shoulders against the open gates; and, while their comrades engaged and overcame the daring spirits among the enemy who struggled to resist, the heavy doors were swung together, and Hougoumont was saved! Immediately stone slabs, broken beams, and the remains or wagons and farm implements were heaped against the gate, and then the storm of baffled and impotent rage burst against the outside. In another instant the heavy cross-bar which held the doors together was fixed by Graham, and the blows of hatchet and bayonet beat unavailingly on the solid planks of which the gate was composed.

Long afterwards the imprint of bloody hands upon the gate-post and timbers told the tale of the frantic disappointment and passion of the assailants, which became fiercer as the cries of the hunted Frenchmen still within the yard became gradually silenced in death.

As at Quatre Bras the 42nd Highlanders (the Black Watch) received the French cavalry into the still unformed square, then closing its ranks, turned upon the intruders and exterminated them, so now the Guards at Hougoumont proceeded to dispose of Cubieres' Light Infantry one by one. So fierce now became the pent-up wrath of the baffled enemy that an effort was next made to scale the high brick archway above the gate, and for this purpose a tall French Grenadier, amid the shouts of his comrades, mounted on their shoulders, and leaning over the top, took deliberate aim at Captain Wyndham, who at the moment was holding a musket in one hand while directing Sergeant Graham where to rest a massive beam of wood which Graham had brought to strengthen the gate. Noticing the Frenchman's movement and intention, Wyndham calmly handed the musket to Graham, who was a marksman of note, and with a significant gesture indicated the sharpshooter, whose musket was levelled, and who had merely to draw the trigger. Instantly grasping the situation, Graham took aim and fired. Two shots rang out, but the Frenchman's weapon discharged itself harmlessly in mid-air, and he fell backwards on the heads of his companions, pierced through the brain.

At the same moment the assailants were taken in rear by a force of four companies of the Coldstream Guards under Colonel Alexander Woodford. Woodford's men fixed bayonets and charged. The enemy immediately gave way and withdrew from the contest, which enabled Woodford to enter the farm by a side-door in the lane. Woodford had come at the personal request of Wellington himself to assist Macdonell; but although senior in rank to that gallant officer, he refused to supersede him.

The French continued during the whole of the day to renew their attack, but at no time were they able to enter the farm. As already stated, the attack had begun at half-past eleven; the assault on the great North Gate took place at one o'clock and was succeeded by a series of determined attacks by the whole of Bachelu's Division till three o'clock, when it became apparent to Napoleon that these troops were being thrown away without result, and that now a different line of action must be adopted. He resolved to make the position untenable by setting the whole of the buildings on fire.

Among the two hundred and fifty pieces of artillery which Bonaparte had brought into the field of battle were a number of howitzers, which he directed to be formed into a powerful battery in order that their fire might be concentrated upon the chateau and farm. It was not long ere the projectiles thrown among the inflammable materials accumulated in the farm caused them to burst into flame. The great barn, filled, as we have seen, with wounded Guardsmen, was the first to catch fire; then followed the outhouses on the north side of the chateau and the farmer's house; and, finally, the chateau itself burned furiously.

Amid dense volumes of black smoke, which attracted the attention of the combatants far and near producing a temporary lull in the general engagement the roofs of these buildings were seen to fall in, in quick succession, sending vast sheets of flame upwards, with brilliant effect. It speaks well of the discipline of the defenders that, although many of the Guardsmen had brothers and kinsmen lying wounded within the burning buildings, it was recognised by all that the defence of their various posts was the first duty of each man, and not one left his rank, terrible as was the anxiety to save the wounded, until the permission of the officer in command had first been obtained.

It was at this moment that Sergeant Graham, whose post was now at the hastily improvised *banquette* composed of benches, tables, chairs, and other like materials, appealed to Colonel Macdonell to allow him to withdraw from the fighting-line. Macdonell consented; but he asked Graham, whose bravery was well known to him, why he should retire when matters were at such a critical point. 'I would not,' said Graham, 'only my brother lies wounded in that building which has just caught fire.'

Leave was cheerfully granted; and Graham, laying down his musket, ran into the blazing building, lifted his brother to a place of safety in a ditch close by, and was back at his post almost instantly. Graham's wounded brother survived to thank his commanding officer, who in his turn repeatedly expressed his admiration for the high sense of duty and the brotherly affection shown by these lads from County Monaghan.

Nor did Macdonell forget the sergeant's gallant behaviour; for when the Duke of Wellington awarded the Norcross bequest of five hundred pounds to Colonel Macdonell as 'the bravest soldier at Waterloo,' it was to Graham that he passed on the gift, with the remark, 'I cannot claim all the merit due to the closing of the gates of Hougoumont; for Sergeant John Graham, who saw with me the importance of the step, rushed forward, and together we shut the gates.'

Battle of Mont St. Jean
a French report

Battle of Mont St. Jean

At nine in the morning, the rain having somewhat abated, the first corps put itself in motion, and placed itself with the left on the road to Brussels, and opposite the village of Mont St. Jean, which appeared the centre of the enemy's position. The second corps leaned its right upon the road to Brussels, and its left upon a small wood, within cannon-shot of the English army. The cuirassiers were in reserve behind, and the guards in reserve upon the heights. The sixth corps, with the cavalry of General D'Aumont, under the order of Count Lobau, was destined to proceed in the rear of our right to oppose a Prussian corps, which appeared to have escaped Marshal Grouchy, and to intent to fall upon our right flank; an intention which had been made known to us by our reports, and by the letter of a Prussian general, enclosing an order of battle, and which was taken by our light troops.

The troops were full of ardour. We estimated the force of the English army at eighty thousand men. We supposed that the Prussian corps, which might be in line towards the right, might be fifteen thousand men. The enemy's force then was upwards of ninety thousand men; our's less numerous.

At noon, all the preparations being terminated, Prince Jerome, commanding a division of the second corps, and destined to form the extreme left of it, advanced upon the wood of which the enemy occupied a part. The cannonade began. The enemy supported, with thirty pieces of cannon, the troops he had sent to keep the wood. We made also, on our side, dispositions of artillery. At one o'clock, Prince Jerome was master of all the wood, and the whole English army fell back behind a curtain. Count D'Erlon then attacked the village of Mont St. Jean, and supported his attack with eighty pieces of cannon, which must have occasioned great loss to the English army. All our efforts were made on the opposite eminence. A brigade of the first division of Count D'Erlon took the village of Mont St. Jean; a second brigade was charged by a corps of English cavalry, which occasioned it much loss. At the same moment a division of English cavalry charged the battery of Count D'Erlon by its right, and disorganized several pieces; but the cuirassiers of General Milhaud charged that division, three regiments of which were broken and cut up.

It was three in the afternoon. The emperor made the guard advance to place it in the plain upon the ground which the first corps had occupied at the outset of the battle; this corps being ready in advance. The Prussian division whose movement had been foreseen, then engaged with the light troops of Count Lobau, spreading its fire upon our whole right flank. It was expedient, before undertaking any thing elsewhere, to wait for the event of this attack. Hence, all the means in reserve were ready to succour Count Lobau, and overwhelm the Prussian corps when it should have advanced.

This done, the emperor had the design of leading an attack upon the village of Mont St. Jean, from which we expected decisive success; but, by a movement of impatience, so frequent in our military annals, and which has often been so fatal to us, the cavalry of reserve having perceived a retrograde movement made by the English to shelter themselves from our batteries, from which they had suffered so much, crowned the heights of Mont St. Jean, and charged the infantry. This movement, which, made in proper time, and supported by the reserves, must have decided the day, made in an isolated manner, and, before the affair on the right was terminated, became fatal.

Having no means of countermanding it, the enemy showed many masses of cavalry and infantry, and our two divisions of cuirassiers being engaged, all our cavalry ran at the same moment to support their comrades. There, for three hours, numerous charges were made, which enables us to penetrate several squares, and to take six standards of the light infantry, an advantage out of proportion with the loss which our cavalry experienced by the grape-shot and musket-firing. It was impossible to dispose of our reserves of infantry until we had repulsed the flank-attack of the Prussian corps. This attack always prolonged itself perpendicularly upon our right flank. The emperor sent thither General Dehesme with the young guard, and several batteries of reserve. The enemy was kept in check, repulsed, and fell back—he had exhausted his forces and we had nothing more to fear. This was the moment that indicated for an attack upon the centre of the enemy. As the cuirassiers had suffered by the grape-shot, we sent four battalions of the middle-guard to protect them, to keep the position, and, if possible, disengage and draw back into the plain a part of our cavalry.

Two other battalions were sent to keep themselves in force upon the extreme left of the division, which had manoeuvred upon our flanks, in order not to have any uneasiness on that side—the rest was disposed in reserve, part to occupy the eminence in rear of Mont St. Jean, and part upon the ridge in rear of the field of battle, which formed our position of retreat.

In this state of affairs, the battle was gained; we occupied all the positions, which the enemy had possessed at the outset of the battle. Our cavalry having been too soon and ill employed, we could no longer hope for decisive success; but Marshal Grouchy, having learned the movement of the Prussian corps, marched upon the rear of it, ensured us a signal success on the next day. After eight hours' fire and charges of infantry and cavalry, all the army saw with joy the victory gained, and the field of battle in our power.

At half-after eight o'clock, the four battalions of the middle guard, who had been sent to the ridge on the other side of Mont St. Jean, to support the cuirassiers, being greatly annoyed by the grape- shot, endeavoured to carry the batteries with the bayonet. At the end of the day, a charge directed against their flank, by several English squadrons, put them in disorder. The fugitives re-crossed the ravine. Several regiments, which were near at hand, seeing some troops belonging to the guard in confusion, believed it was the old guard, and, in consequence, fled in disorder. Cries of *All is lost, the guard is driven back*, were heard on every side. The soldiers even pretended that on many points ill-disposed persons cried out, *Save who can*. However this may be, a complete panic at once spread itself throughout the whole field of battle, and the troops threw themselves in the greatest disorder on the line of communication; soldiers, cannoniers, caissons, all pressed to this point; the old guard, which was in reserve, was infected, and was itself hurried along.

In an instant, the whole army was nothing but a mass of confusion; all the soldiers, of all arms, were mixed *pêle-mêle*, and it was utterly impossible to form a single corps. The enemy, who perceived this astonishing confusion, immediately attacked with their cavalry, and increased the disorder; and such was the confusion, owing to night coming on, that it was impossible to rally the troops, and point out to them their error. Thus terminated the battle, a day of false manoeuvres was rectified, the greatest success ensured for the next day, yet all was lost by a moment of panic terror. Even the body-guard drawn up by the side of the emperor, was disorganized and overthrown by an overwhelming force, and there was then nothing else to be done but to follow the torrent. The parks of reserve, all the baggage which had not re-passed the Sambre, in short every thing that was on the field of battle, remained in the power of the enemy. It was impossible to wait for the troops on our right; every one knows what the bravest army in the world is when thus mixed and thrown into confusion, and when its organization no longer exists.

The emperor crossed the Sambre at Charleroi, at five o'clock in the morning of the 19th. Philippeville and Avesnes have been given as the points of reunion. Prince Jerome, General Morand, and other generals, have there already rallied a part of the army. Marshal Grouchy, with the corps on the right, is moving on the lower Sambre.

The loss of the enemy must have been very great, if we may judge from the number of standards we have taken from them, and from the retrograde movements which they have made;—ours cannot be calculated till after the troops shall have been collected. Previous to the confusion which took place, we had already experienced a very considerable loss, particularly in our cavalry, so fatally, though so bravely, engaged. Notwithstanding these losses, this brave cavalry constantly kept the position it had taken from the English, and only abandoned it when the tumult and disorder of the field of battle forced it. It the midst of the night, and the obstacles which encumbered their route, it could not preserve its organization.

The artillery was as usual covered with glory. the carriages belonging to the head-quarters remained in their ordinary position; no retrograde movement being judged necessary. In the course of the night they fell into the enemy's lands.

Such was the result of the battle of Mont St. Jean, so glorious for the French armies, and yet so fatal.

Marshal Ney's Account
from a letter to the
Duke of Otranto

Marshal Ney's Account

M. Le Duc

The most false and defamatory reports have been publicly circulated for some days, respecting the conduct which I have pursued during this short and unfortunate campaign. The journals have repeated these odious calumnies, and appear to lend them credit. After having fought during twenty-five years for my country, and having shed my blood for its glory and independence, an attempt is made to accuse me of treason; and maliciously to mark me out to the people, and the army itself, as the author of the disaster it has just experienced.

Compelled to break silence, while it is always painful to speak of oneself, and particularly to repel calumnies, I address myself to you, sir, as the president of the provisional government, in order to lay before you a brief and faithful relation of the events I have witnessed. On the 11th of June, I received an order from the minister of war to repair to the imperial head-quarters. I had no command, and had no information upon the force and composition of the army. Neither the emperor nor his minister had given me any previous hint, from which I could anticipate that I should be employed in the present campaign; I was consequently taken unprepared, without horses, without equipage, and without money; and I was obliged to borrow the necessary expenses of my journey. I arrived on the 12th at Laon, on the 13th at Avesnes, and, on the 14th, at Beaumont. I purchased, in this last city, two horses from the Duke of Treviso, with which I proceeded on the 15th, to Charleroi, accompanied by my first aide-de-camp, the only officer I had with me. I arrived at the moment when the enemy, attacked by our light troops, was retreating upon Fleurus to Gosselies.

The emperor immediately ordered me to put myself at the head of the first and second corps of infantry, commanded by Lieutenant-Generals d'Erlon and Reille, of the divisions of light cavalry of Lieutenant-General Pire, of the division of light cavalry of the guard under the command of Lieutenants-General Lefebvre Desnouettes and Colbert, and of two divisions of cavalry of Count Valmy, forming altogether eight divisions of infantry and four of cavalry. With these troops, a part of which only I had as yet under my immediate command, I pursued the enemy, and formed him to evacuate Gosselies, Frasne, Millet, and Heppiegnies. There I took up a position for the night, with the exception of the first corps, which was still at Marchiennes, and which did not join me until the following day.

On the 16th, I was ordered to attack the English in their position at Les Quatre Bras. We advanced towards the enemy with an enthusiasm difficult to be described. Nothing could resist our impetuosity. The battle became general, and victory was no longer doubtful; when, at the moment that I intended to bring up the first corps of infantry, which had been left by me in reserve at Frasne, I learned that the emperor had disposed of it, without acquainting me of the circumstance, as well as of the division of Girard of the second corps, that he might direct them upon St. Amand, and to strengthen his left wing, which was warmly engaged with the Prussians. The shock which this intelligence gave me confounded me. Having now under my command only three divisions, instead of the eight upon which I calculated, I was obliged to re-nounce the hopes of my victory; and, in spite of all my efforts, notwithstanding the intrepidity and devotion of my troops, I could not do more than maintain myself in my position till the close of the day. About nine o'clock, the first corps was returned to me by the emperor, to whom it had been of no service. Thus twenty-five or thirty thousand men were absolutely paralyzed, and were idly paraded, during the whole of the battle, from the right to the left, and the left to the right, without firing a shot.

I cannot help suspending these details for a moment, to call your attention to all the melancholy consequences of this false movement, and, in general, of the bad disposition during the whole of the day. By what fatality, for example, did the emperor, instead of directing all his forces against Lord Wellington, who would have been taken unawares, and could not have resisted, consider this attack as secondary? How could the emperor, after the passage of the Sambre, conceive it possible to fight two battles on the same day? It was to oppose forces double ours, and to do what the military men who were witnesses of it can scarcely yet comprehend. Instead of this, he had left a corps of observation to watch the Prussians, and marched with his most powerful masses to support me, the English army would undoubtedly have been destroyed between Les Quatre Bras and Gemappe; and that position, which separated the two allied armies, being once in our power, would have afforded the emperor an opportunity of outflanking the right of the Prussians, and of crushing them in their turn. The general opinion in France, and especially in the army, was, that the emperor would have bent his whole efforts to annihilate first the English army; and circumstances were favourable for the accomplishment of such a project: but fate ordered it otherwise.

On the 17th, the army marched in the direction of Mont St. Jean.

On the 18th, the battle commenced at one o'clock, and

though the bulletin which details it makes no mention of me, it is not necessary for me to say that I was engaged in it. Lieutenant-General Count Drouet has already spoken of that battle in the chamber of peers. His narration is accurate, with the exception of some important facts which he has passed over in silence, or of which he was ignorant, and which it is now my duty to disclose. About seven o'clock in the evening, after the most dreadful carnage which I have ever witnessed, General Labedoyere came to me with a message from the emperor, that Marshal Grouchy had arrived on our right, and attacked the left of the united English and Prussians. This general officer, in riding along the lines, spread this intelligence among the soldiers, whose courage and devotion remained unshaken, and who gave new proofs of them at that moment, notwithstanding the fatigue with which they were exhausted. What was my astonishment, (I should rather say indignation,) when I learned, immediately afterwards, that, so far from Marshal Grouchy having arrived to our support, as the whole army had been assured, between forty and fifty thousand Prussians were attacking our extreme right, and forcing it to retire!

Whether the emperor was deceived with regard to the time when the marshal could support him, or whether the advance of the marshal was retarded by the efforts of the enemy longer than was calculated upon, the fact is, that at the moment when his arrival was announced to us, he was still only at Wavre upon the Dyle, which to us was the same as if he had been a hundred leagues from the field of battle.

A short time afterwards, I saw four regiments of the middle guard advancing, led on by the emperor. With these troops he wished to renew the attack, and to penetrate the centre of the enemy. He ordered me to lead them on. Generals, officers, and soldiers, all displayed the greatest intrepidity; but this body of troops was too weak long to resist the forces opposed to it by the enemy, and we were soon compelled to renounce the hope which this attack had for a few moments inspired. General Friant was struck by a ball at my side, and I myself had my horse killed, and fell under it. The brave men who have survived this terrible battle, will, I trust, do me the justice to state, that they saw me on foot, with sword in hand, during the whole of the evening, and that I was one of the last who quitted the scene of carnage at the moment when retreat could no longer be prevented. At the same time, the Prussians continued their offensive movements, and our right sensibly gave way. The English also advanced in their turn. There yet remained to us four squares of the old guard, to protect our retreat. These brave grenadiers, the flower of the army, forced successively to retire, yielded ground foot by foot, until finally overpowered by numbers, they were almost completely destroyed. From that moment the retrograde movement was decided, and the army formed nothing but a confused mass. There was not, however, a total rout, nor the cry of *Save who can*, as has been calumniously stated in the bulletin. As for myself, being constantly in the rear-guard, which I followed on foot, having had all my horses killed, worn out with fatigue, covered with contusions, and having no longer strength to walk, I owe my life to a corporal, who supported me in the march, and did not abandon me during the retreat. At eleven at night, I met Lieutenant-General Lefebvre Desnouettes; and one of his officers, Major Schmidt, had the generosity to give me the only horse that remained to him. In this manner I arrived at Marchienne-au-Pont, at four o'clock in the morning, alone, without any officers of my staff, ignorant of the fate of the emperor, of whom, before the end of the battle, I had entirely lost sight, and who, I had reason to believe, was either killed or taken prisoner. General Pamphile Lacroix, chief of the staff of the second corps, whom I found in this city, having told me that the emperor was at Charleroi, I supposed that his majesty intended to place himself at the head of Marshal Grouchy's corps, to cover the Sambre, and to facilitate to the troops the means of rallying near Avesnes; and with this persuasion I proceeded to Beaumont; but parties of cavalry following us too closely, and having already intercepted the roads of Maubeuge and Philippeville, I became sensible of the total impossibility of arresting a single soldier on that point to oppose the progress of the victorious enemy. I continued my march upon Avesnes, where I could obtain no intelligence concerning the emperor.

In this state of things, having no intelligence of his majesty, nor of the major-general the disorder increasing every instant, and, with the exception of some veterans of the regiments of the guard and of the line, every one pursuing his own inclination, I determined to proceed immediately to Pris by St. Quentin, and disclose, as quickly as possible, the true state of affairs to the minister of war, that he might send some fresh troops to meet the army, and rapidly adopt the measures which circumstances required. At my arrival at Bourget, three leagues from Paris, I learned that the emperor had passed through that place at nine o'clock in the morning.

Such, M. le Duc, is a faithful history of this calamitous campaign.

I now ask those who have survived that fine and numerous army, how I can be accused of the disasters of which it has been the victim, and of which our military annals furnish no example. I have, it is said, betrayed my country—I who, to serve it, have shewn a zeal which I have perhaps carried too far; but this calumny is not and cannot be supported by any fact or any presumption. Whence have these odious reports, which spread with frightful rapidity, arisen? If, in the inquiries which I have made on this subject, I had not feared almost as much to discover as to be ignorant of the truth, I should declare that every circumstance proves that I have been basely deceived, and that it is attempted to cover, under the veil of treason, the errors and extravagancies of this campaign; error which have not been avowed in the bulletins that have appeared, and against which I have in vain raised that voice of truth which I will yet cause to resound in the chamber of peers. I expect from the justice of your excellency, and from your kindness to me, that you will cause this letter to be inserted in the journals, and give it the greatest possible publicity.

I renew to your excellency, &c.

Marshal Prince of the Moskwa

Paris, June 26th, 1815

What the Gordons Did at Waterloo

from the journal of
Sergeant Robertson

What the Gordons Did at Waterloo

THE ROAD TO QUATRE BRAS

On the 26th of January 1815, we marched to Cork again with the intention of embarking for Scotland but, owing to certain circumstances we were detained until the 1st or May when, instead of embarking for our native country, we were ordered off to Belgium again to take up our quarters in the tented field. We weighed anchor on the 3rd and on the 8th landed at Ostend and disembarked next day. We halted here and got three days' rations served out which we managed to get cooked. In the evening we embarked on board the boats on the canal and proceeded to Ghent, where we arrived on the 11th at daybreak.

It happened to be the weekly market day when we landed, and none of us ever saw such a sight before. The day was beautiful, and the people were coming in boats from all directions to the centre of the city, which caused great stir and bustle; and to add to the effect of the scene, we were disembarked at the large market-place. If the novelty of what we saw made an impression on our minds, the Belgians were no less surprised at our strange appearance as, I believe, none of them had ever seen any clad in the Highland garb before.

We were all regularly billeted upon the inhabitants without distinction, and were civilly used by them. In a few days we were joined by the Royal Scots, 42nd, and 79th, and were pleased at meeting with so many Scotchmen, more especially those brave fellows with whom we had fought side by side in Egypt and Denmark, at Corunna, Fontes, and Vittoria; among the Pyrenees, at Bayonne and Toulouse.

We remained in Ghent till the 28th of the month, without the occurrence of anything worthy of notice, when we marched to Brussels, where the Duke of Wellington had his headquarters, and were put in divisions under the command of Sir Thomas Picton, Sir James Kempt, and Sir Denis Pack. When we came to Alast, half way between Ghent and Brussels, we found the Duke de Berri commanding a body of French troops that adhered to the Bourbon cause. Almost all the officers had served in the French army in Spain, and some of them had been in Egypt. The latter upon seeing the Highland regiments, immediately came running to meet us, and asked very kindly if 'they had not seen us before?' When we answered in the affirmative, they went and told the Duke, who expressed his happiness to have such supporters to aid the cause of his house.

On our arrival at Brussels we were billeted throughout the city. The 28th, 32nd, 34th, 95th, and two battalions of the Hanoverian militia joined us here, which were paraded in brigade every second day. While here we had a grand review, which was attended by all the resident Belgian and English nobility. Recruiting for the Belgian army was going on with great activity, and hundreds daily marched to the different depots. They were mostly all good-looking young fellows and had a very soldier-like appearance. We were now served with four days' bread, and supplied with camp kettles, bill hooks and everything necessary for a campaign, which according to all accounts was fast approaching. The inhabitants, like those of Ghent, were very civil and kind to us, and we in turn were the same to them. We were kept in a state of alarm for some days from reports that appeared in the Belgian papers to the effect that the French troops were moving on to the frontiers.

In order to avoid being taken unawares, the orderly sergeants were desired to take a list of the men's quarters, with the names of the streets, and the numbers of the houses. It was also arranged that every company and regiment should be billeted in the same or the adjacent streets to prevent confusion if called out at a moment's warning.

On the evening of the 15th of June, the sergeants on duty were all in the orderly room till ten o'clock at night; and no orders having been issued, we went home to our quarters. I had newly lain down in bed when the bugle sounded the alarm, the drums beat to arms, bagpipes played and all was in commotion, thus stunning the drowsy ear of night by all kinds of martial music sounding in every street. Upon hearing this, sergeants and corporals ran to the quarters of their respective parties to turn them out. I went to the quartermaster for bread and four days' allowance was given out of the store, which was soon distributed among the men, every one getting his share and speedily falling into rank. So regular and orderly was the affair gone about, that we were ready to march in half an hour after the first sound of the bugle.

Colonel Cameron had that day been invested with the Order of the Bath by the title of Sir John Cameron of Fassifearn and was present at a splendid ball given by the Duchess of Richmond, daughter of the seventh Duke of Gordon who was brother to the Marquis of Huntly. She had invited some sergeants of the 92nd to show the company especially the Belgians, the Highland reel and sword dance, which they did. When the alarm sounded, the Duke of Wellington was quickly at our head and we commenced our march at daybreak, leaving the city by the Lamour gates, followed by the inhabitants to whom we gave three farewell cheers.

When we had got a few miles from Brussels we entered a wood, the trees of which were remarkably tall, and although the road was very wide it was wet and soft, as the sun did not strike upon it to make it dry. During our march we had several times to diverge to the right and left, to avoid the bad parts of the road. When we had got a good way into the wood we met a number of wagons conveying Prussian soldiers who had been wounded the day before, who told us that the French were driving all before them, and that we were greatly needed. As we were too apt to entertain bad opinions, we suspected treachery on the part of the foreigners, and that we should have to retreat; for we did not credit much what the Prussians told us of the affair.

We continued our route until we came to the skirt of the wood, into which we were marched, and ordered to lie down and rest ourselves for two hours, but not to kindle any fires, and on no account to move out of our places We lay down and slept for some time, when the Duke of Wellington and his staff rode by, which made us move, but we were not called upon to march. While lying here we were joined by a great many Hanoverians and Brunswickers. When we emerged into open ground, we found ourselves at the village of Waterloo. About eleven o'clock we fell in and marched on.

The day was oppressively warm and the road very dusty. We moved on slowly till we reached the village of Geneppe, where the inhabitants had large tubs filled with water standing at the doors, ready for us, of which we stood in great need. They told us that a French *patrole* had been there that morning. We had hardly got out of the town when we heard the sound of cannon at no great distance which proceeded from the place where the conflict was going on between the French and the Belgians. The sound had a stimulating effect upon us; for so eager were we to enter the field of action, that we felt as fresh as if we had newly started. In fact we were all anxious to assist the poor Belgians, who were but young soldiers, and consequently little experienced in military affairs. 'Forward,' was now the word that ran through all the ranks;

but the Colonel had more discretion, and would not allow us to run, lest we should exhaust ourselves before the time. He issued peremptory orders that every man should keep his rank as if on parade, and not march above three miles an hour. The firing seemed to be coming nearer as we approached a farm and public-house, called Quatre Bras.

THE TERRIBLE BATTLE OF QUATRE BRAS

We now went off the road to the left of the house and closed up upon the front division in columns of battalions ready to form line. Before many minutes had elapsed, we received some shots from the French artillery which galled us considerably, as we had none up yet to return the compliment. The French made a movement to their own right; and the 42nd and 79th were ordered to oppose them, in a field on which was growing a crop of long wheat or rye. As those regiments were moving on to take possession of a wood to the left, a little in front of our position, they were attacked by a strong body of cavalry, which made considerable havoc among them. The 92nd was now brought to the front of the farmhouse and formed on the road, with our backs to the walls of the building and garden, our right resting upon the crossroads, and our left extending down the front. We were ordered to prime and load and sit down with our firelocks in our hands, at the same time keeping in line. The ground we occupied rose with a slight elevation, and was directly in front of the road along which the French were advancing.

Shortly after we had formed here the Duke of Wellington and his staff came and dismounted in rear of the centre of our regiment, and ordered the grenadier company to wheel back on the left and the light company on the right; so that the walls of the house and garden in our rear with the eight companies in front, joined in a square, in case any or the enemy's cavalry should attack us. We had not been long in this way, when a column of Brunswick hussars, with the Duke of Brunswick at their head, made a charge down the road on the right. In this, however, they were unsuccessful, and were driven back with considerable loss, the Duke being among the slain. The column of French cavalry that drove back the Brunswickers retired a little, then re-formed, and prepared to charge our regiment; but we took it more coolly than the Brunswickers did. When the Duke of Wellington saw them approach, he ordered our left wing to fire to the right, and the right wing to fire to the left, by which we crossed the fire; and a man and horse affording such a large object for an aim, very few of them escaped. The horses were brought down and the riders, if not killed, were made prisoners. Some of them had the audacity to draw their swords upon the men when in the act of taking them, but such temerity only served to accelerate their own destruction; for in the infuriated state of mind in which we were at the moment, those guilty of such conduct fared a worse fate than those who submitted without a murmur.

We were informed by the prisoners that Napoleon himself was in the field, so were also our old friends Soult and Ney; and that Ney was directly in our front, and had ordered a charge to be made upon us. We were very happy on hearing this intelligence, as the thought that the two great generals of the time were to meet each other on the field of battle, stimulated us to do our utmost to maintain unsullied the hard-earned reputation which the British army had gained in many a bloody battle field.

As far as I am aware this was the first time that ever the Emperor had been personally engaged with us and we were anxious to know if the same good fortune which attended his former campaigns still awaited him, and whether he would be able to re-enact the splendid achievements of Lodi, Marengo, and Austerlitz, when brought into the arena against an army for the most part composed of veteran troops, and command-ed by brave and experienced generals. We wished to show him that we were made of sterner stuff than those whom he was wont to chase over the length and breadth of Europe.

Immediately after the enemy's cavalry had been driven back and partially destroyed, a column of infantry was sent round to a wood on our right and another to push us in front. At this time the 30th, 69th, and 73rd regiments joined us, upon which we left our ground to charge down the road, led by General Barnes and Colonel Cameron. Just as we had taken our stand, a volley was fired at the Duke of Wellington from behind a garden hedge. As I was the first sergeant he observed on turning round, he ordered me to take a section and drive them out. I accordingly got a section and we went into the garden when, after a short contest, we succeeded in driving them out, after having killed a good many of them. By the time I got out of the garden and came to the road the regiment was closely engaged with the bayonet. The lieuten-ant-colonel at this time was coming up as fast as he could ride having been shot through the groin. We immediately joined the regiment at the foot of the garden and advanced at full speed, the French having by this time given way. In the im-petuosity of our charge we had advanced too near the en-emy's guns and were obliged to move off to the right to the skirts of the wood. We then advanced rapidly on the right and turned the left flank of the French.

We now made a determined attack to seize two of the en-emy's guns, which gave us considerable annoyance, but were foiled in the attempt. At this time the Guards came up and the action began to be general. We, however, still sustained considerable loss from the enemy's cannon, as we had none with which to oppose them; and as so few of our troops had come up, we could not form a sufficiently strong column in one place to enable us to take any of their artillery from them. Our regiment was now very much cut up both in officers and men, as we had been first in the action and, with the other Highland regiments had for a long time to resist the attack of the whole French army. We continued very warmly engaged until about eight o'clock in the evening, when we rallied, and made another effort to capture the enemy's guns. In this attempt I received a wound in the head, while in the act of cheering the men forward. I was very sick for a short time, and was sent to the rear under the care of the surgeon, where I got my wound dressed, and remained till morning; when I awoke I found I was able to join the regiment again. On account of this wound I was reported dead and my old companions were rather surprised at my return. On calling over the roll the night previous, it was found that we had lost one colonel, one major, four captains, twelve lieutenants, four ensigns, twelve sergeants, and about 250 rank and file.

The regiment was now formed in the rear of the house of Quatre Bras. Before we had time to cook our victuals the Duke of Wellington and his staff came into the midst of us and gave orders for the march of the different divisions. The cavalry by this time were coming up in great strength; and on the arrival of General Hill at their head we all stood up and gave him three hearty cheers, as we had long been under his command in the Peninsula, and loved him dearly on account of his kind and fatherly conduct towards us. When he came among us he spoke in a very kindly manner and inquired concerning our welfare. He also expressed his sorrow that the colonel was wounded; and gave us a high character to the Duke of Wellington who replied that he knew what we could do and that by-and-bye he would give us something to keep our hands in use. We now removed as many of the wounded out of the field as we could and buried all the dead bodies within our reach, especially the officers.

After remaining here till about ten o'clock we fell back to the skirts of a wood near the village of Waterloo, the cavalry forming our rear guard. The French now pushed very hard upon us, but we still managed to keep the road. On coming to the village of Genappe, we found the houses were full of our wounded who had made that length and were not able to go any further. When the French came up they were all taken prisoners. We now heard that Colonel Cameron had died on the road about an hour before we came to Genappe. We still kept moving very slowly, until the French artillery got close to our rear, and were annoying us very much, when the Duke ordered a regiment of Hanoverian infantry to wait and assist our cavalry, who were formed on each side of the road, to protect our flanks which they effectually did.

We arrived at length at the house of Le Hay Saint, a very large building having a great entrance gate on the left hand, where the Brussels road is cut through a small green hill with high banks on each side. On coming to the rear of the house we diverged to the right and left. The right of Sir Thomas Picton's division to which we belonged, rested on the great road; and the left extended on in rear of a double hedge that is two hedges with a bye-road running between them. It had been raining very hard ever since we commenced our march in the morning and we were drenched to the skin. The ground on which we were formed had been lately ploughed and the corn was newly sprouting above the ground, so that with the number of men that were treading upon it, the field was reduced to the consistency of mortar. However, we formed line, and the French halted opposite to us much in the same state. The weather soon began to fair up, but still everything round and below was very wet. We now thought of getting our muskets in order for action, for by every appearance we were likely to need them soon. I took the opportunity of going into the hedge to look at the French forming; but such numerous columns I had never looked on before, nor do I believe any man in the British army had ever seen such a host. I must confess that, for my own part, when I saw them taking up their ground in such a regular manner, and everything appearing so correct about all their movements, I could not help wishing that we had had more troops with which to oppose the thousands that were collecting in our front.

Our artillery and a rocket-brigade had now arrived, all the cavalry had come up, and a great number of foreign infantry had already joined us. The evening at length cleared but without any sunshine. We had a fine view of the country round the village of Mount St Jean which stood within half a mile of our rear, and the skirts of the great forest of Soignes lay not much farther off. We could get no fuel here to make fires as everything was soaked with the rain. There was a field of green clover in our rear of which we cut large quantities, and with some branches out of the hedges made a kind of bed on the ground to keep us from the clay. Every regiment sent to its own front a small picquet for the purpose or giving information to the commanding officer in case of alarm. In this condition we stretched ourselves on our uncomfortable lair.

We lay till about twelve o'clock when the alarm was given that the French were coming. We instantly stood to our arms and continued in that posture until the cause of the alarm was found to be groundless; it arose from a part of the Belgian cavalry going their rounds, having when challenged by our sentries replied in the French language. During all this time it continued to rain very hard. As we had lain down by fours, we had blankets enough to cover us and keep us dry; but when we got up again we were made as wet as before. The place on which we lay was like a marsh and for the season of the year the rain was very cold. Notwithstanding all these disagreeable circumstances, we lay down again and slept sound, as we were very much fatigued.

We were aroused by daybreak on the morning of the 18th and ordered to stand to our arms, till the line should be reconstructed. During the time I never felt colder in my life; every one of us was shaking like an aspen leaf. An allowance of gin was then served out to each of us which had the effect of infusing warmth into our almost inanimate frames, as before we got it, we seemed as if under a fit of ague. We remained on the ground till about six o'clock, when we were ordered to clean ourselves, dry our muskets, try to get forward, and commence cooking. We had scarcely got breakfast discussed when a shot from the French killed one of our pioneers who was sleeping. We were now ordered to stand to our arms, prime and load, fix bayonets, wheel into line, and be ready to act in any manner required. By this time the action had begun on the right, and the Duke and his staff had taken up their position on the green height in the rear of Le Hay Saint, where he could see the whole of the line from right to left. Beyond the hedge in our front was a fallow field, having a gentle ascent towards it; and being placed rather in rear of the slope, the French cannoniers could not hit us with their shot, but they made some shells to bear upon us, which made great havoc in our ranks. As yet we had not fired a shot but what had been discharged by our outposts.

The French were now busy in forming columns to their own right, which was directly in our front, and we were expecting every moment to be attacked, as all on the right of our division were warmly engaged. We were well cautioned to be steady and keep together, as, in all likelihood, we would be first attacked by cavalry, who would try to break our line; and, above all, to mind what word of command was given whether to form square or whatever else the order might be. At this time, our men were falling fast from the grape shot and shells that the French were pouring in among us, while as yet we had not discharged a musket.

The artillery attached to us had now commenced a brisk fire, which drew a great deal of the French fire upon our ranks, as we were immediately in rear of the artillery. At length a large column of French infantry was seen advancing in our direction. Everyone was now eager to be led on, and as the way they were taking indicated that it was upon that part of the line where the 92nd was stationed that the attack would be made, General Pack ordered us to advance and line the hedge to oppose the advance of the column. But when we got to the side of the hedge we found the French were there as soon as we. We cheered loudly, and called to the Scotch Greys, who were formed up in our rear, 'Scotland for ever!' Upon which, some person in the regiment called out 'charge' when, all at once, the whole regiment broke through the hedge, and rushed headlong on the French column.

The onset was so sudden and unexpected, that it threw them into confusion. At this critical moment, the Greys flew like a whirlwind to our assistance, and having got round on the flanks of the column, they placed themselves between the enemy and our own line. While we pushed them hard in front the other cavalry regiments in the brigade, the Royals, Blues, and Enniskillen Dragoons, came at full speed to our aid, when it was fearful to see the carnage that took place. The dragoons were lopping off heads at every stroke, while the French were calling for quarter. We were also among them busy with the bayonet and what the cavalry did not execute we completed; but, owing to the position taken up by the dragoons, very few of the French escaped. It was here that some of the 92nd and the Greys had a struggle for the eagle which a sergeant of the Greys bore off.

In this charge all the sergeants and one of the officers at the colours were killed. So terrible was the havoc which the Greys had made, and such the fearful impression that they produced on the minds of the French, that nothing was heard from those among them who were literally trodden down but appeals to deliver them from those dragoons. A poor fellow cried out to me to save him, and he would give me his watch and all his money; but being called to the colours I was obliged to leave him. One of our regiment, however, fortunately came to the place where he was, and as he spoke in good English, our fellow thought he was a Briton and conducted him to the rear. We now returned to our old ground as we could not retain possession of what we had acquired.

When we had resumed our old station we found that we had lost a great many in the late affair, and among those that had fallen, was my particular and well-beloved comrade, Sergeant-Major Taylor. As I knew he had a valuable watch upon him, I went out between the fires of the two lines and took it and some other things off him, for the behoof of his widow. We had not time as yet to ascertain the amount of our loss, but I found that our captain had been wounded, and was amissing and that I was left in command of two companies, as we lost all the subaltern officers on the 16th. On the right of our division the French cavalry were making a dreadful push, and we often thought that they would force their way through our lines, but the firm and determined resistance of our troops at last convinced them that their efforts were unavailing.

After the charge already mentioned we were not troubled for a long time nor did we fire any for two hours. During all this time however, we suffered much from the enemy's artillery. We were ordered to sit down and rest ourselves. During this intermission, we had a fine view of what was passing on the right. I could see the French cavalry make those terrible charges which frequently drove ours to the rear, but when our men came to the forest, they faced about and beat them back in turn. And often, when the French cavalry were compelled to pull about, our infantry gave them a dreadful volley on the way when passing. It was, I suppose, at this stage of the action that the French account of the battle stated that they took possession of Mount St Jean; but, in truth, they did not keep it for one minute, as from where we were seated I had a perfect sight of what was going forward. At this time, the 27th and 40th regiments had arrived from Brussels and were forming column in front of the large farmhouse, on the outside of the village. Although the French cavalry had obtained possession of the village, it would have been impossible for them to have retained it while our cavalry had the support of these regiments.

About four o'clock the enemy made another attack on our part of the line, by a large body of lancers, who rode up to our squares with as much coolness as if subjecting us to a regimental inspection. We kept up a smart fire upon them, however, and put them to the right about. But before we had succeeded in turning them they did us considerable damage by throwing their lances into our columns, which, being much longer than the firelock and bayonet, gave them a great advantage over us.

At this time we could distinctly see large columns of infantry forming in our front, with numerous bodies of artillery, and we expected we were to be called upon to sustain a charge from all kinds of arms. We were again ordered to line our old hedge to be in readiness to receive them. When we saw the dense masses collecting in our front ready to rush upon us we looked for nothing but that our line would be broken, and utter discomfiture would be the consequence. The bodies of our artillerymen lay beside the guns which they had so bravely managed and many a cannon had not a gunner left to discharge it. At this time there was scarcely an officer left in our regiment, in consequence of which the command of the company devolved upon me. I now began to reflect on what should be done in case of a retreat becoming inevitable, over a long plain, in front of cavalry. I was aware it would be difficult for me to keep the men together, as they had never retreated before under similar circumstances. In fact, any word of command misunderstood in the smallest degree would be sure to produce disorder. And in the face of peril so imminent, there must always be some persons more afraid than others, whose timidity might infect the rest; whereas, when advancing to meet the enemy every one becomes emboldened and confusion is not so likely to occur.

While we were in this state, with life and death in the balance, the French column began to move forward. An awful pause ensued. Every man, however, was steady. At length they came within pistol-shot of our lines, when a volley of rockets was let off by the brigade that had been formed in the hedge, which threw them into entire confusion. To complete their disorder we, at the same instant, gave a loud huzza and poured a well-directed volley upon them. This unexpected and rather rough reception made them turn round and run, leaving behind them a number of killed and wounded.

When this brush was over, we sent out a few skirmishers in our front along the hedge, merely to keep up the fire, and give information of what was passing among the French, who were still keeping up a distant cannonade. We now opened our files along the hedge, as the wider they were kept, there was less danger to be apprehended from the round shot, and in this way we remained for a long time. Notwithstanding this precaution they were occasionally taking oft some of us.

It was now seven o'clock and by this time there was no officer in the regiment but the commanding officer (whose horse had been shot), the adjutant, and very few sergeants. I had charge of two companies, and was ordered to pay particular attention to any signal or movement I might see in front, for which purpose I was furnished with a spy-glass.

In a short time one of our skirmishers came running in, and called to me to look at the French lines, as something extraordinary was going on. On the enemy's right I saw that a cross fire had been commenced, and that troops in the same dress had turned the extremity of their line and were advancing rapidly. I immediately informed the adjutant, who said that perhaps it was a mutiny in the French army, and that we had better form our companies close so as to be ready to march to any point. At this instant an aide-de-camp came galloping down our rear, and calling out, 'The day is our own the Prussians have arrived.'

All eyes were now turned to the right to look for the signal to charge which was to be given by the Duke of Wellington. Nothing could stop our men, and it was only by force that the non-commissioned officers could keep them from dashing into the French lines. No language can express how the British army felt at this time; their joy was truly ecstatic.

By this time the aide-de-camp had returned to the Duke who was standing in the stirrups with his hat elevated above his head. Every eye was fixed upon him, and all were waiting with impatience to make a finish of such a hard day's work. At last he gave three waves with his hat and the loud three cheers that followed the signal were the heartiest that had been given that day. On seeing this, we leapt over the hedge that had been such a protection to us during the engagement and in a few minutes we were among the French lines. Nothing was used now but the bayonet, for, after the volley we gave them, we set off at full speed, and did not take time to load. All was now destruction and confusion.

The French at length ran off throwing away knapsacks, firelocks, and every thing that was cumbersome, or that could impede their flight. One division at the farm house of La Belle Alliance made an attempt to stand, and came to the charge. When the three Highland regiments saw the resistance offered by this column, we rushed upon it like a legion of demons. Such was our excited and infuriated state of mind at the time, and being flushed with thought of victory we speedily put an end to their resistance. The Prussians were now among us the one nation cheering on the other, while the bands were playing their national anthems.

It was now dark, and we were ordered to halt for the night, while the Prussians marched past us. The place where we bivouacked was immediately at the end of the house where Bonaparte had stood all day, which was by this time filled with the wounded. As we had not got any water during the day numbers of us went in search of it. After looking about for some time, we at length discovered a draw-well and accordingly supplied ourselves. The next morning I looked into the well and discovered that it was full of dead bodies; but as we were not aware of this circumstance when we drank the water we never felt any bad effects from using it.

In fact, we were not in a condition to quarrel about the quality of the liquid we got as a cup of water of almost any kind was considered a boon by our unfortunate wounded comrades, who were suffering that insatiable and dreadful thirst which is experienced by men in their situation. The night was now far advanced and as we could not see what was going on at a distance we lay down to repose ourselves, cherishing the fond hope that as we had now vanquished the enemy, we would be permitted to sleep in peace.

When morning came, I arose and went out to view the field on which so many brave soldiers had perished. The scene which then met my eyes was horrible in the extreme. The number of the dead was far greater than I had ever seen on any former battle field. The bodies were not scattered over the ground but were lying in heaps men and horses mixed promiscuously together. It might truly have been called the ' crowning carnage,' for death had indeed been here and had left visible evidences of his grim presence in the misery and devastation that surrounded us. I turned away with disgust from this heart-melting spectacle, and had scarcely arrived at my quarters when every person that could be spared was sent out to carry the wounded to the roadside, or any other convenient place where the wagons could be brought to convey them to the hospital.

We had not proceeded far in this humane duty when we were ordered to make ready and at seven o'clock marched to the right to get on to the great road that leads to Paris. At any other time we would have hailed the order with joy but a very different feeling now pervaded our minds. When we thought that we were called to leave the place where so many of our brave companions were lying, without either seeing the dead interred or the wounded taken proper care of, our hearts were filled with grief and vexation. Numbers who had fought by our side on the preceding day were now stretched lifeless on the open field; and we were not permitted to give them the common rites and see them decently interred in the field where they had spent their heart's blood. I confess my feelings overcame me; I wept bitterly and wished I had not been a witness of such a scene.

The following is a list of the killed and wounded belonging to the 92nd, on the 16th and 18th days of June 1815, at Quatre Bras and Waterloo:

June 16th, at Quatre Bras	June 18th, at Waterloo
1 colonel	1 major
2 captains	4 captains
14 lieutenants	4 ensigns
2 ensigns	1 surgeon
3 sergeants	10 sergeants
61 rank and file	298 rank and file

Total of killed and wounded on both days, 402

Having at last got on the great road to Paris, we had not marched many miles from the field when we took some prisoners from whom we learned that Napoleon had set off for Paris. There was not an inhabitant to be seen, all having fled to the woods. We halted near a small village for the night, when the Duke of Wellington in person came up and thanked us for the manner in which we had conducted ourselves during the engagement, and lavished the highest eulogiums upon us for our exertions to uphold the reputation of the British army. But he had one fault to find with the 92nd, and that was for being so forward in crossing the hedge in the early part of the action. He said, as it turned out all was well; but had it happened otherwise it might have ruined all his plans, and caused the destruction of the whole left wing of the army; and he urged upon us to pay attention to the words of command that might be issued next day. He then galloped off to pay his respects to the other regiments who had been similarly engaged.

* * * * * *

Medals were awarded to us but some disagreeable feeling was likely to arise, when we heard that there was to be a difference in the material of which they were to be made. We were told that officers were to receive gold medals, while those for the privates were to be composed of brass, which partiality nearly caused a mutiny. At length, when the Duke of Wellington learned the dissatisfaction that prevailed, he ordered that they should be all alike, that as we had all shared equally of the dangers of the day we should all partake alike of its glories.

Sergeant Lawrence at Waterloo
from the autobiography of
Sergeant William Lawrence
of the 40th Regiment of Foot

Sergeant Lawrence at Waterloo

On the 17th of June, 1815, we marched through Brussels, amid the joy of the inhabitants, who brought us out all manner of refreshments. I heard some remarks from them to the effect that we were all going to be slaughtered like bullocks, but we only laughed at this, telling them that that was nothing new to us. Some of the younger recruits, however, were terribly downcast and frightened at the idea of fighting, but I have often found that it is these most timid ones who when they come to an actual battle rush forward and get killed first; probably owing to the confused state they are in, while the more disciplined soldiers know better what course to pursue.

From Brussels we marched to about five or six miles out of the town, not far from the village of Waterloo, when our commander sent his aide-decamp to Lord Wellington for general orders how he was to act, or as to what part of the line we were to fall in at. The orders returned were that we were to stay in our present position till next morning, so that night we crept into any hole we could find, cowsheds, cart-houses, and all kinds of farmstead buildings, for shelter, and I never remember a worse night in all the Peninsular war, for the rain descended in torrents, mixed with fearful thunder and lightning, and seeming to foretell the fate of the following morning, the 18th, which again happened to be Sunday.

The allied army had on the 16th and 17th been attacked by Napoleon's large forces at Ligny and Quatre Bras, but neither side had obtained any great success, beyond thousands being killed on both sides; during the night of the 17th, therefore, firing was continually going on, which I could distinctly hear, in spite of its being considerably drowned by the thunder. All that night was one continued clamour, for thousands of camp-followers were on their retreat to Brussels, fearful of sticking to the army after the Quatre Bras affair. It was indeed a sight, for owing to the rain and continued traffic the roads were almost impassable, and the people were sometimes completely stuck in the mud: and besides these a continual stream of baggage-wagons was kept up through the night.

Early in the morning of the 18th we were again put on the march to join our lines, our position being in the reserve, which included the Fourth and Twenty-Seventh Regiments, together with a body of Brunswickers and Dutch, and formed a line between Merk Braine and Mont St. Jean on the Brussels road. Our regiment took the left of this road, but did not remain there long, for the French were seen in motion, and on their opening fire from their cannon we soon marched up to action in open column.

During this movement a shell from the enemy cut our deputy-sergeant-major in two, and having passed on to take the head off one of *my* company of grenadiers named William Hooper, exploded in the rear not more than one yard from me, hurling me at least two yards into the air, but fortunately doing me little injury beyond the shaking and carrying a small piece of skin off the side of my face. It was indeed another narrow escape, for it burnt the tail of my sash completely off, and turned the handle of my sword perfectly black. I remember remarking to a sergeant who was standing close by me when I fell, "This is sharp work to begin with, I hope it will end better:" and even this much had unfortunately so frightened one of the young recruits of my company, named Bartram, who had never before been in action and now did not like the curious evolutions of this shell so close to him, that he called out to me and said he must fall out of rank, as he was taken very ill.

I could easily see the cause of his illness, so I pushed him into rank again, saying, "Why, Bartram, it's the smell of this little powder that has caused your illness; there's nothing else the matter with you;" but that physic would not content him at all, and he fell down and would not proceed another inch. I was fearfully put out at this, but was obliged to leave him, for if he had had his due he ought to have been shot. From this time I never saw him again for at least six months, but even then I did not forget him for this affair of cowardice.

The right of our line had been engaged some little time before we were ordered up, and then our position was changed, we having to cross the road and proceed to the right of a farmhouse called La Haye Sainte. Owing to the rain that had been peppering down the whole night and even now had not quite ceased, the fields and roads were in a fearful state of dirt and mud, which tended to retard our progress greatly as well as to tire us. It made it very bad too for the action of cavalry, and even more so for artillery.

About ten o'clock the action of the day began at Hougoumont on our right, and from there it fell on our centre, where we were attacked by a tremendous body of cavalry and infantry. "The fire, however, which had been kept up for hours from the enemy's cannon had now to be abated in that quarter, owing to the close unison of the two armies. And from this time onward we endured some heavy work throughout the day, having constantly to be first forming square to receive the repeated attacks of their cavalry, and then line to meet their infantry, charge after charge being made upon us, but with very little success. At the commencement the commanding officer was killed by a musket-shot, but his place was soon filled up.

On our left on the turnpike road was placed a brigade of German cavalry with light horses and men. When Buonaparte's Bodyguards came up they charged these, making fearful havoc amongst their number, they were routed and obliged to retreat, but the Life Guards and Scotch Greys fortunately making their appearance immediately, some close handwork took place, and the Bodyguards at last finding their match, or even more, were in their turn compelled to fall back before the charge of our cavalry, numbers of them being cut to pieces.

Still nothing daunted, they formed again, and this time ascended at us; but of the two, they met with a worse reception than before, for we instantly threw ourselves into three squares with our artillery in the centre; and the word having been given not to fire at the men, who wore armour, but at the horses, which was obeyed to the very letter, as soon as they arrived at close quarters we opened a deadly fire, and very few of. them wholly escaped. They managed certainly at first to capture our guns, but they were again recovered by the fire of our three squares; and it was a most laughable sight to see these Guards in their chimney-armour trying to run away after their horses had been shot from under them, being able to make very little progress, and many of them being taken prisoners by those of our light companies who were out skirmishing. I think this quite settled Buonaparte's Bodyguards, for we saw no more of them, they not having expected this signal defeat.

That affair, however, had only passed off a very few minutes before their infantry advanced and we had again to form line ready to meet them. We in our usual style let the infantry get well within our musket-shot before the order was given to fire, so that our volley proved to be of fearful success: and then immediately charging them we gave them a good start back again, but not without a loss on our side as well as on theirs. And no sooner had they disappeared than another charge of cavalry was made, so that we again had to throw ourselves into square on our old ground. These cavalry had no doubt expected to appear amongst us before we could accomplish this, but fortunately they were mistaken, and our persistent fire soon turned them. We did not lose a single inch of ground the whole day, though after these successive charges our numbers were fearfully thinned, and even during the short interval between each charge the enemy's cannon had been doing some mischief among our ranks besides.

The men in their tired state were beginning to despair, but the officers cheered them on continually throughout the day with the cry of "Keep your ground, my men!" It is a mystery to me how it was accomplished, for at last so few were left that there were scarcely enough to form square.

About four o'clock I was ordered to the colours. This, although I was used to warfare as much as any, was a job I did not at all like; but still I went as boldly to work as I could. There had been before me that day fourteen sergeants already killed and wounded while in charge of those colours, with officers in proportion, and the staff and colours were almost cut to pieces. This job will never be blotted from my memory although I am now an old man, I remember it as if it had been yesterday. I had not been there more than a quarter of an hour when a cannon-shot came and took the captain's head clean off. This was again close to me, for my left side was touching the poor captain's right, and I was spattered all over with his blood.

One of his company who was close by at the time, cried out, "Hullo, there goes my best friend."

Which caused a lieutenant, who quickly stepped forward to take his place, to say to the man, "Never mind, I will be as good a friend to you as the captain."

The man replied, "I hope not, sir."

The officer not having rightly understood his meaning, the late captain having been particularly hard on him for his dirtiness, giving him extra duty and suchlike as punishment. This man, whose name was Marten, was a notorious character in the regiment, and I was myself tolerably well acquainted with him, for he had once been in my company; but on account of the same thing, dirtiness in his person, he had been transferred to this the fifth company, where neither this poor captain had been able to reform him, try however hard he might. Still he was for all this an excellent soldier in the field.

But now I must get on to the last charge of cavalry, which took place not very long after this. Few as we were, when we saw it coming we formed squares and awaited it Then we poured volley after volley into them, doing fearful execution, and they had to retire at last before the strong dose we administered, not, however, without our losing more men and so becoming even weaker than before. We were dreading another charge, but all the help we got was the cry of "Keep your ground, my men, reinforcements are coming!"

Not a bit, however, did they come till the setting sun, in time to pursue our retreating enemy; the Prussians under Marshal Blucher having been detained elsewhere, and although long expected, only being able at this period to make their appearance at last.

I must say here that I cannot think why those charges of cavalry were kept up against our unbroken squares, in spite of their being so constantly sent back. It is murder to send cavalry against disciplined infantry unless they have artillery to act in conjunction with them, in which case they might possibly succeed in routing them if they could take advantage of their falling into confusion, but not otherwise.

We were indeed glad to see the arrival of these Prussians, who now coming up in two columns on our left flank, advanced on the enemy's right. Lord Wellington, who was ever enticing his army on, now came up to our regiment and asked who was in command. On being told it was Captain Brown, he gave the order to advance, which we received with three cheers, and off we set as if renewed with fresh vigour. The attack was now being made by the whole line, together with the Prussians, who had come up fresh and were therefore more than a match for the harassed French. They soon forced the French into a downright retreat by their fire, and the retreat becoming universal, the whole body of the French were thrown into disorder and pursued off the field by Blucher's fresh and untired infantry and cavalry.

We followed them ourselves for about a mile, and then encamped on the enemy's ground; and if ever there was a hungry and tired tribe of men, we were that after that memorable day of the 18th of June. Then the first thing to be thought of was to get a fire and cook some food, which was not so easy, as wood was scarce and what there was was wet through. One of our company, named Rouse, who went out in search of sticks, came across one of the enemy's powder-wagons that we had taken in the battle amongst the rest of the many things, and immediately commenced cutting the cover up for fuel; but his hook coming in contact with a nail or some other piece of iron and striking fire, as a natural consequence the remains of the powder in the wagon exploded and lifted the poor fellow to a considerable height in the air. The most remarkable thing was that he was still alive when he came down and able to speak, though everything had been blown from him except one of his shoes. He was a perfect blackguard, for although he was in a most dangerous state he did not. refrain from cursing his eyes, which happened, as it was, to be both gone, and saying what a fool he must have been. He was that night conveyed to Brussels Hospital with the rest of the many wounded, and died in a few days, raving mad.

We succeeded, however, in getting a fire at last, and then as I happened that night to be orderly sergeant to our general I went and reported myself to him. He was at the time sitting on a gun-carriage holding his horse, and when he saw me, said, "That's right, sergeant; I expect two more sergeants directly, but I wish you would meanwhile try and get some corn for my poor horse."

Off I went accordingly, and found two bushels or so in a sack which had evidently been left by the enemy, as it was on one of their cannon. When I opened the sack I found to my great surprise that it likewise contained a large ham and two fowls, so I asked the general if he would accept them; he, however, declined, saying he would take the corn, but that I might keep the meat for myself, advising me, however, to keep it out of sight of the Prussians, who were a slippery set of men and very likely to steal it if they saw it.

I prepared the hanger for the pot as quickly as possible, putting cross-sticks over the fire at a sufficient distance to prevent them igniting; but before I had finished doing this a quantity of these same Prussians whom the general had been watching and warned me against passed by, and two of them coming to my fire to light their pipes noticed the ham, and remarked that it looked good. I thought it best to take my sword and immediately cut them off a piece each, and they relieved my fears by going off seemingly quite satisfied. They were evidently on the march following up the French, for the whole night we could hear the distant sound of cannon and musketry from the French and Prussians, Lord Wellington having completely given up the pursuit to Marshal Blucher.

I pretty quickly put my ham in the pot after that, and the two sergeants coming up, I set them to pick the fowls, and these soon going in after the ham, in two hours were pretty well done. About this time I heard a Frenchman groaning under a cannon, where he was lying on a quantity of straw. I thought he was badly wounded, and perhaps as hungry as myself, so I went to him and told him as well as I was able to stop till our supper was cooked, and then I would bring him some; but when it was ready and I had cut off some bread, fowl, and ham, and taken it to the place where I had seen him, he had gone. For one reason I was not sorry, for he left his straw, which made a very good bed for us three sergeants, the ground itself being unpleasantly wet I think perhaps this Frenchman must have been a skulker, or he would not have ventured to escape.

We sat down ourselves, however, and made a very good meal off our ham and poultry, and I can safely say we enjoyed our mess as much as men ever did, for I, for one, had had nothing to eat since early in the morning up to that time. After that, as the general did not want us for anything, we retired to rest on our straw, but I was too tired to go to sleep for a long time, and lay contemplating the scenes of the day. I was merely scratched on the face myself during the whole day, besides being a little shaken by the bursting of the shell I mentioned; but this scratch had been terribly aggravated by a private who had been standing next to me having over-printed his musket, with the consequence that when he fired, my face being so close, the powder flew up and caught my wound, which though only originally a slight one soon made me dance for a time without a fiddle.

Of the general loss on that blood-stained day I am unable to give an exact account, but it must have been enormous on both sides, for three hundred of my regiment alone were missing; and this was not so great a loss as that of some regiments, for the one on our right lost six hundred, chiefly from the continual fire of shot and shell that the French cannon had kept up between the charges. But now there was very little delay; and early next morning we were again put in motion, to prevent our enemy, if possible, from getting any breathing time. The Prussians were at least twelve hours in advance of us, so that we really had not much to fear, but still some doubt was entertained as to whether the enemy would make another stand in their own territory, and in all probability such would have been the case if Blucher had not been pushing so close on their heels. I very much doubt, too, if, had not the Prussians come up when they did, both armies would not have remained on the field of Waterloo, and perhaps have joined battle again in the morning, for the French had been expecting fresh reinforcements after their defeat; but these not arriving and we being increased in numbers, no resource was left them but to retreat.

Captain Gronow at Waterloo
1st Regiment of Foot Guards

by Rees Howell Gronow

Captain Gronow at Waterloo

Two battalions of my regiment had started from Brussels; the other (the 2nd), to which I belonged, remained in London, and I saw no prospect of taking part in the great events which were about to take place on the Continent. Early in June I had the honour of dining with Colonel Darling, the deputy adjutant-general, and I was there introduced to Sir Thomas Picton, as a countryman and neighbour of his brother, Mr. Turbeville, of Evenney Abbey, in Glamorganshire. He was very gracious, and, on his two aides-de-camp—Major Tyler and my friend Chambers, of the Guards—lamenting that I was obliged to remain at home, Sir Thomas said:

"Is the lad really anxious to go out?" Chambers answered that it was the height of my ambition. Sir Thomas inquired if all the appointments to his staff were filled up; and then added, with a grim smile, "If Tyler is killed, which is not at all unlikely, I do not know why I should not take my young countryman: he may go over with me if he can get leave."

I was overjoyed at this, and, after thanking the General a thousand times, made my bow and retired.

I was much elated at the thoughts of being Picton's aide-de-camp, though that somewhat remote contingency depended upon my friends Tyler, or Chambers, or others, meeting with an untimely end; but at eighteen on *ne doute de rien*. So I set about thinking how I should manage to get my outfit, in order to appear at Brussels in a manner worthy of the aide-de-camp of the great General.

As my funds were at a low ebb, I went to Cox and Greenwood's, those staunch friends of the hard-up soldier. Sailors may talk of the "little cherub that sits up aloft," but commend me for liberality, kindness, and generosity, to my old friends in Craig's Court. I there obtained £200., which I took with me to a gambling-house in St. James' Square, where I managed, by some wonderful accident, to win £600.; and, having thus obtained the sinews of war, I made numerous purchases, amongst others two first-rate horses at Tattersall's for a high figure, which were embarked for Ostend, along with my groom.

I had not got leave; but I thought I should get back, after the great battle that appeared imminent, in time to mount guard at St. James's. On a Saturday I accompanied Chambers in his carriage to Ramsgate, where Sir Thomas Picton and Tyler had already arrived; we remained there for the Sunday, and embarked on Monday in a vessel which had been hired for the General and suite. On the same day we arrived at Ostend, and put up at an hotel in the square; where I was surprised to hear the General, in excellent French, get up a flirtation with our very pretty waiting-maid.

Sir Thomas Picton was a stern-looking, strong-built man, about the middle height. He generally wore a blue frock-coat, very tightly buttoned up to the throat; a very large black silk neck-cloth, showing little or no shirt-collar; dark trousers, boots, and a round hat: it was in this very dress that he was attired at Quatre Bras, as he had hurried off to the scene of action before his uniform arrived.

After sleeping at Ostend, the General and Tyler went the next morning to Ghent, and on Thursday to Brussels. I proceeded by boat to Ghent, and, without stopping, hired a carriage, and arrived in time to order rooms for Sir Thomas at the Hotel d'Angleterre, Rue de la Madeleine, at Brussels: our horses followed us.

While we were at breakfast, Colonel Canning came to inform the General that the Duke of Wellington wished to see him immediately. Sir Thomas lost not a moment in obeying the order of his chief, leaving the breakfast-table and proceeding to the park, where Wellington was walking with Fitzroy Somerset and the Duke of Richmond. Picton's manner was always more familiar than the Duke liked in his lieutenants, and on this occasion he approached him in a careless sort of way, just as he might have met an equal.

The Duke bowed coldly to him, and said, "I am glad you are come, Sir Thomas; the sooner you get on horseback the better; no time is to be lost. You will take the command of the troops in advance. The Prince of Orange knows by this time that you will go to his assistance."

Picton appeared not to like the Duke's manner; for, when he bowed and left, he muttered a few words which convinced those who were with him that he was not much pleased with his interview.

QUATRE BRAS

I got upon the best of my two horses, and followed Sir Thomas Picton and his staff to Quatre Bras at full speed. His division was already engaged in supporting the Prince of Orange, and had deployed itself in two lines in front of the road to Sombref when he arrived. Sir Thomas immediately took the command. Shortly afterwards, Kempt's and Pack's brigades arrived by the Brussels road, and part of Alten's division by the Nivelles road.

Ney was very strong in cavalry, and our men were constantly formed into squares to receive them. The famous Kellerman, the hero of Marengo, tried a last charge, and was very nearly being taken or killed, as his horse was shot under him when very near us. Wellington at last took the offensive; a charge was made against the French, which succeeded, and we remained masters of the field. I acted as a mere spectator, and got, on one occasion, just within twenty or thirty yards of some of the cuirassiers; but my horse was too quick for them.

On the 17th, Wellington retreated upon Waterloo, about eleven o'clock. The infantry were masked by the cavalry in two lines, parallel to the Namur road. Our cavalry retired on the approach of the French cavalry, in three columns, on the Brussels road. A torrent of rain fell, upon the Emperor's ordering the heavy cavalry to charge us; while the fire of sixty or eighty pieces of cannon showed that we had chosen our position at Waterloo. Chambers said to me:

"Now, Gronow, the loss has been very severe in the Guards, and I think you ought to go and see whether you are wanted; for, as you have really nothing to do with Picton, you had better join your regiment, or you may get into a scrape."

Taking his advice, I rode off to where the Guards were stationed; the officers—amongst whom I remember Colonel Thomas and Brigade-Major Miller—expressed their astonishment and amazement on seeing me, and exclaimed:

"What the deuce brought you here? Why are you not with your battalion in London? Get off your horse, and explain how you came here!"

Things were beginning to look a little awkward, when Gunthorpe, the adjutant, a great friend of mine, took my part and said:

"As he is here, let us make the most of him; there's plenty of work for everyone. Come, Gronow, you shall go with the Hon. Captain Clements and a detachment to the village of Waterloo, to take charge of the French prisoners."

"What the deuce shall I do with my horse?" I said. Upon which the Hon. Captain Stopford, aide-de-camp to Sir John Byng, volunteered to buy him.

Having thus once more become a foot soldier, I started

according to orders, and arrived at Waterloo with a detachment, under Captain Clements, brother of Lord Leitrim, to
take charge of some hundreds of French prisoners. They had
been taken at Quatre Bras, and were confined in a barn and
the courtyard of a large farm-house. As ill-luck would have it,
Clements did not place sentinels on the other side of the wall,
which overlooked the plain leading to the forest of Soignies;
the consequence was, that with the aid of a large wagon,
which had been left in the yard, several of the prisoners scaled
the wall, and made their escape. As soon as it was night, some
more poor fellows attempted to follow their example; but
this time the alarm was given and our men fired and killed or
wounded a dozen of them.

This firing at so late an hour brought several officers of the
staff from the neighbouring houses to ascertain the cause, and
among them came my poor friend Chambers, who kindly
invited me to Sir Thomas Picton's quarters to supper. I accompanied him thither, and after groping our way into the
house, for it was very dark, we passed the door of a room in
which Sir Thomas himself was lying. I heard him groan, from
the pain of the wound he had received at Quatre Bras, but did
not of course venture to disturb him, and we passed on into a
small hall, where I got some cold meat and wine.

General Appearance of the
Field of Waterloo

The day on which the battle of Waterloo was fought seemed
to have been chosen by some providential accident for which
human wisdom is unable to account. On the morning of the
18th the sun shone most gloriously, and so clear was the at-
mosphere that we could see the long, imposing lines of the

enemy most distinctly. Immediately in front of the division to which I belonged, and, I should imagine, about half a mile from us, were posted cavalry and artillery; and to the right and left the French had already engaged us, attacking Huguemont and La Haye Sainte. We heard incessantly the measured boom of artillery, accompanied by the incessant rattling echoes of musketry.

The whole of the British infantry not actually engaged were at that time formed into squares; and as you looked along our lines, it seemed as if we formed a continuous wall of human beings. I recollect distinctly being able to see Bonaparte and his staff; and some of my brother officers using the glass, exclaimed, "There he is on his white horse." I should not forget to state that when the enemy's artillery began to play on us, we had orders to lie down, when we could hear the shot and shell whistling around us, killing and wounding great numbers; then again we were ordered on our knees to receive cavalry. The French artillery—which consisted of three hundred guns, though we did not muster more than half that number—committed terrible havoc during the early part of the battle, whilst we were acting on the defensive.

THE BATTLE OF WATERLOO

At daylight, on the 18th, we were agreeably surprised to see a detachment of the 3rd Guards, commanded by Captain Wigston and Ensign George Anson, son of the lamented General who died in India, who had been sent to relieve us. I took the opportunity of giving Anson, then a fine lad of seventeen, a silver watch, made by Barwise, which his mother, Lady Anson, had requested me to take over to him. Bob Clements and I then proceeded to join our regiment.

The road was ankle-deep in mud and slough; and we had not proceeded a quarter of a mile when we heard the trampling of horses' feet, and on looking round perceived a large cavalcade of officers coming at full speed. In a moment we recognised the Duke himself at their head. He was accompanied by the Duke of Richmond, and his son, Lord William Lennox. The entire staff of the army was close at hand: the Prince of Orange, Count Pozzo di Borgo, Baron Vincent, the Spanish General Alava, Prince Castel Cicala, with their several aides-de-camp; Felton Harvey, Fitzroy Somerset, and Delaney were the last that appeared. They all seemed as gay and unconcerned as if they were riding to meet the hounds in some quiet English county.

In about half-an-hour we joined our comrades in camp, who were endeavouring to dry their accoutrements by the morning sun, after a night of rain and discomfort in their bivouac. I was now greeted by many of my old friends (whom I had not had time to speak to the day before, when I was sent off to the village of Waterloo) with loud cries of "How are you, old fellow? Take a glass of wine and a bit of ham? it will perhaps be your last breakfast."

Then Burges called out, "Come here, Gronow, and tell us some London news."

He had made himself a sort of gipsy-tent, with the aid of some blankets, a Sergeant's halberd and a couple of muskets. My dear old friend was sitting upon a knapsack, with Colonel Stuart, (who afterwards lost his arm,) eating cold pie and drinking champagne, which his servant had just brought from Brussels. I was not sorry to partake of his hospitality, and, after talking together some time, we were aroused by the drums beating to arms. We fell in, and the muster-roll having been called, the piling of arms followed; but we were not allowed to leave our places.

The position taken up by the British army was an excellent one: it was a sort of ridge, very favourable for artillery, and from which all the movements of the French could be discerned. In case of any disaster, Wellington had several roads in his rear by which a masterly retreat could have been effected through the forest on Brussels; but our glorious commander thought little about retreating: on the contrary, he set all his energies to work, and determined to win the day.

Our brigade was under the orders of General Maitland, and our division was commanded by Sir George Cooke. We occupied the right centre of the British line, and had the château of Hougoumont at about a quarter of a mile's distance on our right. Picton was on the extreme left at La Haye Sainte, with his division of two British and one Hanoverian brigades. Hougoumont was garrisoned by the 2nd and 3rd regiments of the Guards, a battalion of Germans, and two battalions of artillery, who occupied the *château* and gardens. Between each regiment was a battery of guns, and nearly the whole of the cavalry was to the left of Sir Thomas Picton's division.

About half-past eleven the bands of several French regiments were distinctly heard, and soon after the French artillery opened fire. The rapid beating of the *pas de charge,* which I had often heard in Spain—and which few men, however brave they may be, can listen to without a somewhat unpleasant sensation—announced that the enemy's columns were fast approaching. On our side the most profound silence prevailed, whilst the French, on the contrary, raised loud shouts, and we heard the cry of *"Vive l'Empereur!"* from one end of their line to the other.

The battle commenced by the French throwing out clouds of skirmishers from Hougoumont to La Haye Sainte. Jerome Bonaparte's division, supported by those of Foy and Bachelu, attacked Hougoumont, the wood and garden of which were taken and retaken several times; but, after prodigies of valour performed on both sides, remained in the hands of the French: who, however, sustained immense loss, and the château still belonged to the invincible English Guards.

Whilst the battle was raging in the wood and orchard, eighty French guns, mostly twelve-pounders, opened upon us, and caused a heavy loss in our ranks. At the same moment, we could perceive from our elevated position that the enemy were attacking La Haye Saint in great force. At about two o'clock, Ney, with the first corps formed in four columns, advanced *en échelon* the left wing forward. They completely defeated and put to flight a Dutch-Belgian brigade, and then attacked Picton's division. He, however, made a desperate resistance, and charged them several times, though they were four times his number. It was then that noble soldier was killed by a musket-ball. Things looked ill there; when the Duke ordered up Adam's brigade, which regained the ground, and pushed eagerly forward.

At the same time Lord Uxbridge commanded the cavalry to charge. This order was admirably executed by Somerset on one side, and by Ponsonby on the other, and was for a time completely successful. The French infantry brigades of Quiot, Donzelot, and Marcoguet were rolled up and almost annihilated; twenty guns were dismantled or spiked, and many hundred prisoners taken; several squadrons of cuirassiers were also charged and put to the rout. Unfortunately our cavalry went too far without proper supports, and were charged and driven back by Milhaud's heavy cavalry and Jacquinot's lancers, and had to take refuge behind our own lines. Ney now received orders to attack La Haye Sainte, which was taken about four o'clock. At the same hour Bulow's first columns made their appearance, and attacked D'Erlon and Lobau.

The Guards had what in modern battues is called a hot corner of it, and the greatest "gluttons" (and we had many such) must have allowed, when night came on, that they had had fighting enough. I confess that I am to this day astonished that any of us remained alive. From eleven o'clock till seven we were pounded with shot and shell at long and short range, were incessantly potted at by *tirailleurs* who kept up a most biting fire, constantly charged by immense masses of cavalry who seemed determined to go in and win, preceded as their visits were by a terrific fire of artillery; and, last of all, we were attacked by *"la Vieille Garde"* itself. But here we came to the end of our long and fiery ordeal. The French veterans, conspicuous by their high bearskin caps and lofty stature, on breasting the ridge behind which we were at that time, were met by a fearful fire of artillery and musketry, which swept away whole masses of those valiant soldiers; and, while in disorder, they were charged by us with complete success, and driven in utter rout and discomfiture down the ravine. The Prussians having now arrived in force on the French right, a general advance of the whole line was ordered, and the day was won.

During the battle our squares presented a shocking sight. Inside we were nearly suffocated by the smoke and smell from burnt cartridges. It was impossible to move a yard without treading upon a wounded comrade, or upon the bodies of the dead; and the loud groans of the wounded and dying were most appalling.

At four o'clock our square was a perfect hospital, being full of dead, dying, and mutilated soldiers. The charges of cavalry were in appearance very formidable, but in reality a great relief, as the artillery could no longer fire on us: the very earth shook under the enormous mass of men and horses. I never shall forget the strange noise our bullets made against the breastplates of Kellermann's and Milhaud's cuirassiers, six or seven thousand in number, who attacked us with great fury. I can only compare it, with a somewhat homely simile, to the noise of a violent hail-storm beating upon panes of glass.

The artillery did great execution, but our musketry did not at first seem to kill many men; though it brought down a large number of horses, and created indescribable confusion.

The horses of the first rank of cuirassiers, in spite of all the efforts of their riders, came to a stand-still, shaking and covered with foam, at about twenty yards' distance from our squares, and generally resisted all attempts to force them to charge the line of serried steel. On one occasion, two gallant French officers forced their way into a gap momentarily created by the discharge of artillery: one was killed by Staples, the other by Adair. Nothing could be more gallant than the behaviour of those veterans, many of whom had distinguished themselves on half the battle-fields of Europe.

In the midst of our terrible fire, their officers were seen as if on parade, keeping order in their ranks, and encouraging them. Unable to renew the charge, but unwilling to retreat, they brandished their swords with loud cries of *"Vive l'Empereur!"* and allowed themselves to be mowed down by hundreds rather than yield. Our men, who shot them down, could not help admiring the gallant bearing and heroic resignation of their enemies.

The Duke of Wellington in Our Square

About four P.M. the enemy's artillery in front of us ceased firing all of a sudden, and we saw large masses of cavalry advance: not a man present who survived could have forgotten in after life the awful grandeur of that charge. You discovered at a distance what appeared to be an overwhelming, long moving line, which, ever advancing, glittered like a stormy wave of the sea when it catches the sunlight. On they came until they got near enough, whilst the very earth seemed to vibrate beneath the thundering tramp of the mounted host. One might suppose that nothing could have resisted the shock of this terrible moving mass. They were the famous cuirassiers, almost all old soldiers, who had distinguished themselves on most of the battlefields of Europe. In an almost incredibly short period they were within twenty yards of us, shouting *"Vive l'Empereur!"* The word of command, "Prepare to receive cavalry," had been given, every man in the front ranks knelt, and a wall bristling with steel, held together by steady hands, presented itself to the infuriated cuirassiers.

I should observe that just before this charge the duke entered by one of the angles of the square, accompanied only by one aide-de-camp; all the rest of his staff being either killed or wounded. Our commander-in-chief, as far as I could judge, appeared perfectly composed; but looked very thoughtful and pale. He was dressed in a grey great-coat with a cape, white cravat, leather pantaloons, Hessian boots, and a large cocked hat *a la Russe*.

The charge of the French cavalry was gallantly executed; but our well-directed fire brought men and horses down, and ere long the utmost confusion arose in their ranks. The officers were exceedingly brave, and by their gestures and fearless bearing did all in their power to encourage their men to form again and renew the attack. The Duke sat unmoved, mounted on his favourite charger. I recollect his asking the Hon. Lieut.-Colonel Stanhope what o'clock it was, upon which Stanhope took out his watch, and said it was twenty minutes past four. The Duke replied:

"The battle is mine; and if the Prussians arrive soon, there will be an end of the war."

The French Cavalry Charging
the Brunswickers

Soon after the cuirassiers had retired, we observed to our right the red hussars of the *Garde Imperiale* charging a square of Brunswick riflemen, who were about fifty yards from us. This charge was brilliantly executed, but the well-sustained fire from the square baffled the enemy, who were obliged to retire after suffering a severe loss in killed and wounded. The ground was completely covered with those brave men, who lay in various positions, mutilated in every conceivable way. Among the fallen we perceived the gallant colonel of the hussars lying under his horse, which had been killed, All of a sudden two riflemen of the Brunswickers left their battalion, and after taking from their helpless victim his purse, watch, and other articles of value, they deliberately put the colonel's pistols to the poor fellow's head and blew out his brains. "Shame! shame!" was heard from our ranks, and a feeling of indignation ran through the whole line; but the deed was done: this brave soldier lay a lifeless corpse in sight of his cruel foes, whose only excuse perhaps was that their sovereign, the Duke of Brunswick, had been killed two days before by the French.

Again and again various cavalry regiments, heavy dragoons, lancers, hussars, carabineers of the Guard, endeavoured to break our walls of steel. The enemy's cavalry had to advance over ground which was so heavy that they could not reach us except at a trot; they therefore came upon us in a much more compact mass than they probably would have done if the ground had been more favourable. When they got within ten or fifteen yards they discharged their carbines, to the cry of *"Vive l' Empereur!"* their fire produced little effect, as that of cavalry generally does. Our men had orders not to fire unless they could do so on a near mass; the object being to economize our ammunition, and not to waste it on scattered soldiers. The result was, that when the cavalry had discharged their carbines, and were still far off, we occasionally stood face to face, looking at each other inactively, not knowing what the next move might be. The lancers were particularly troublesome, and approached us with the utmost daring. On one occasion I remember, the enemy's artillery having made a gap in the square, the lancers were evidently waiting to avail themselves of it, to rush among us, when Colonel Staples at once observing their intention, with the utmost promptness filled up the gap, and thus again completed our impregnable steel wall; but in this act he fell mortally wounded. The cavalry seeing this, made no attempt to carry out their original intentions, and observing that we had entirely regained our square, confined themselves to hovering round us. I must not forget to mention that the lancers in particular never failed to despatch our wounded whenever they had an opportunity of doing so.

When we received cavalry, the order was to fire low; so that on the first discharge of musketry the ground was strewed with the fallen horses and their riders, which impeded the advance of those behind them and broke the shock of the charge. It was pitiable to witness the agony of the poor horses, who really seemed conscious of the dangers that surrounded them: we often saw a poor wounded animal raise its head, as if looking for its rider to afford him aid. There is nothing perhaps amongst the episodes of a great battle more striking than the debris of a cavalry charge, where men and horses are seen scattered and wounded on the ground in every variety of painful attitude. Many a time the heart sickened at the moaning tones of agony which came from man and scarcely less intelligent horse, as they lay in fearful agony upon the field of battle.

THE UNFORTUNATE CHARGE OF
THE HOUSEHOLD BRIGADE

When Lord Uxbridge gave orders to Sir W. Ponsonby and Lord Edward Somerset to charge the enemy, our cavalry advanced with the greatest bravery, cut through everything in their way, and gallantly attacked whole regiments of infantry; but eventually they came upon a masked battery of twenty guns, which carried death and destruction through our ranks, and our poor fellows were obliged to give way. The French cavalry followed on their retreat, when, perhaps, the severest hand-to-hand cavalry fighting took place within the memory of man. The Duke of Wellington was perfectly furious that this arm had been engaged without his orders, and lost not a moment in sending them to the rear, where they remained during the rest of the day. This disaster gave the French cavalry an opportunity of annoying and insulting us, and compelled the artillerymen to seek shelter in our squares; and if the French had been provided with tackle, or harness of any description, our guns would have been taken. It is, therefore, not to be wondered at that the Duke should have expressed himself in no measured terms about the cavalry movements referred to. I recollect that, when his grace was in our square, our soldiers were so mortified at seeing the French deliberately walking their horses between our regiment and those regiments to our right and left, that they shouted, "Where are our cavalry? why don't they come and pitch into those French fellows?"

THE LAST CHARGE AT WATERLOO

It was about five o'clock on that memorable day, that we suddenly received orders to retire behind an elevation in our rear. The enemy's artillery had come up en masse within a hundred yards of us. By the time they began to discharge their guns, however, we were lying down behind the rising ground, and protected by the ridge before referred to. The enemy's cavalry was in the rear of their artillery, in order to be ready to protect it if attacked; but no attempt was made on our part to do so. After they had pounded away at us for about half an hour, they deployed, and up came the whole mass of the Imperial infantry of the Guard, led on by the

Emperor in person. We had now before us probably about 20,000 of the best soldiers in France, the heroes of many memorable victories; we saw the bearskin caps rising higher and higher as they ascended the ridge of ground which separated us, and advanced nearer and nearer to our lines. It was at this moment the Duke of Wellington gave his famous order for our bayonet charge, as he rode along the line: these are the precise words he made use of—"Guards, get up and charge!" We were instantly on our legs, and after so many hours of inaction and irritation at maintaining a purely defensive attitude—all the time suffering the loss of comrades and friends—the spirit which animated officers and men may easily be imagined. after firing a volley as soon as the enemy were within shot, we rushed on with fixed bayonets, and that hearty hurrah peculiar to British soldiers.

It appeared that our men, deliberately and with calculation, singled out their victims; for as they came upon the Imperial Guard our line broke, and the fighting became irregular. The impetuosity of our men seemed almost to paralyze their enemies: I witnessed several of the Imperial Guard who were run through the body apparently without any resistance on their parts. I observed a big Welshman of the name of Hughes, who was six feet seven inches in height, run through with his bayonet, and knock down with the butt end of his firelock, I should think a dozen at least of his opponents. This terrible contest did not last more than ten minutes, for the Imperial Guard was soon in full retreat, leaving all their guns and many prisoners in our hands. The famous General Cambronne was taken prisoner fighting hand to hand with the gallant Sir Colin Halkett, who was shortly after shot through the cheeks by a grape-shot. Cambronne's supposed answer of *"La Garde ne se rend pas"* was an invention of after-times, and he himself always denied having used such an expression.

NAPOLEON AT WATERLOO

I am willing to admit that the tide of success had turned against Napoleon, that he was not altogether what he had been, when at Austerlitz and Wagram he carried all before him. Then, flushed with victory, he was animated with the certainty of success, which in itself was an earnest of triumph. But all was changed when the mighty conqueror came to play his last stake on the field of Waterloo. He knew defeat was possible, for he had been vanquished; and, though his prestige was immense, yet the *Garde Imperiale*, and the other veterans of his noble army, who in former days had only thought of victory when commanded by him, now whispered together of dying with him.

Even the bravest of soldiers, or the most desperate of gamblers, plays his last stake with some degree of emotion and hesitation, knowing that all depends on the throw; and Napoleon, feeling that (humanly speaking) he held in his hand the fate of empires, and his own, knew that if he lost the day, all was over with him in this world. He was then not quite his former self; and he certainly committed several errors about the middle of the day, and showed considerable hesitation as to the orders to be given. The chief mistake he made, in my humble opinion, was this: he did not support the brilliant charges of his cavalry, and the tremendous fire of his numerous and well-served artillery, by the general advance of his infantry, until it was too late and his cavalry were annihilated.

BYNG WITH HIS BRIGADE AT WATERLOO

No individual officer more distinguished himself than did General Byng at the battle of Waterloo. In the early part of the day he was seen at Huguemont, leading his men in the thick of the fight; later he was with the battalion in square, where his presence animated to the utmost enthusiasm both officers and men. It is difficult to imagine how this courageous man passed through such innumerable dangers from shot and shell without receiving a single wound. I must also mention some other instances of courage and devotion in officers belonging to this brigade; for instance, it was Colonel MacDonell, a man of colossal stature, with Hesketh, Bowes, Tom Sowerby, and Hugh Seymour, who commanded from the inside the Chateau of Huguemont. When the French had taken possession of the orchard, they made a rush at the principal door of the chateau, which had been turned into a fortress. MacDonell and the above officers placed themselves, accompanied by some of their men, behind the portal and prevented the French from entering. Amongst other officers of that brigade who were most conspicuous for bravery, I would record the names of Montague, the "vigorous Gooch," as he was called, and the well-known Jack Standen.

HUGUEMONT

Early on the morning after the battle of Waterloo, I visited Huguemont, in order to witness with my own eyes the traces of one of the most hotly-contested spots of the field of battle. I came first upon the orchard, and there discovered heaps of dead men, in various uniforms: those of the Guards in their usual red jackets, the German Legion in green, and the French dressed in blue, mingled together. The dead and the wounded positively covered the whole area of the orchard; not less than two thousand men had there fallen. The apple-trees presented a singular appearance; shattered branches were seen hanging about their mother-trunks in such profusion that one might almost suppose the stiff-growing and stunted tree had been converted into the willow: every tree was riddled and smashed in a manner which told that the showers of shot had been incessant. On this spot I lost some of my dearest and bravest friends, and the country had to mourn many of its most heroic sons slain here.

I must observe that, according to the custom of commanding officers, whose business it is after a great battle to report to the Commander-in-Chief, the muster-roll of fame always closes before the rank of captain. It has always appeared to me a great injustice that there should ever be any limit to the roll of gallantry of either officers or men. If a captain, lieutenant, an ensign, a sergeant, or a private, has distinguished himself for his bravery, his intelligence, or both, their deeds ought to be reported, in order that the sovereign and nation should know who really fight the great battles of England. Of the class of officers and men to which I have referred, there were many of even superior rank who were omitted to be mentioned in the public despatches.

Thus, for example, to the individual courage of Lord Saltoun and Charley Ellis, who commanded the light companies, was mainly owing our success at Huguemont. The same may be said of Needham, Percival, Erskine, Grant, Vyner, Buckley, Master, and young Algernon Greville, who at that time could not have been more than seventeen years old. Excepting Percival, whose jaws were torn away by a grape-shot, everyone of these heroes miraculously escaped.

I do not wish, in making these observations, to detract from the bravery and skill of officers whose names have already been mentioned in official despatches, but I think it only just that the services of those I have particularized should not be forgotten by one of their companions in arms.

THE DUKE OF WELLINGTON'S
OPINIONOF CAVALRY

A day or two after our arrival in Paris from Waterloo, Colonel Felton Hervey having entered the dining-room with the despatches which had come from London, the Duke asked:

"What news have you, Hervey?"

Upon which, Colonel Felton Hervey answered, "I observe by the Gazette that the Prince Regent has made himself Captain-General of the Life Guards and Blues, for their brilliant conduct at Waterloo."

"Ah!" replied the Duke, "his Royal Highness is our Sovereign, and can do what he pleases; but this I will say, the cavalry of other European armies have won victories for their generals, but mine have invariably got me into scrapes. It is true that they have always fought gallantly and bravely, and have generally got themselves out of their difficulties by sheer pluck."

MARSHAL EXCELMANN'S OPINION OF
THE BRITISH CAVALRY

Marshal Excelmann's opinion about the British cavalry struck me as remarkably instructive: he used to say:

Your horses are the finest in the world, and your men ride better than any Continental soldiers; with such materials, the English cavalry ought to have done more than has ever been accomplished by them on the field of battle. The great deficiency is in your officers, who have nothing to recommend them but their dash and sitting well in their saddles; indeed, as far as my experience goes, your English generals have never understood the use of cavalry: they have undoubtedly frequently misapplied that important

arm of a grand army, and have never, up to the battle of Waterloo, employed the mounted soldier at
the proper time and in the proper place. The British
cavalry officer seems to be impressed with the con-
viction that he can dash and ride over everything; as
if the art of war were precisely the same as that of
fox-hunting. I need not remind you of the charge of
your two heavy brigades at Waterloo: this charge was
utterly useless, and all the world knows they came
upon a masked battery, which obliged a retreat, and
entirely disconcerted Wellington's plans during the
rest of the day.

Permit me to point out a gross error as regards
the dress of your cavalry. I have seen prisoners so
tightly habited that it was impossible for them to
use their sabres with facility." The French Marshal
concluded by observing—"I should wish nothing
better than such material as your men and horses
are made of; since with generals who wield cavalry,
and officers who are thoroughly acquainted with
that duty in the field, I do not hesitate to say I
might gain a battle.

COLONEL COLQUITT

During the terrible fire of artillery which preceded the repeated charges of the cuirassiers against our squares many shells
fell amongst us. We were lying down, when a shell fell between
Captain (afterwards Colonel) Colquitt and another officer. In
an instant Colquitt jumped up, caught up the shell as if it had
been a cricket ball, and flung it over the heads of both officers
and men, thus saving the lives of many brave fellows.

Captain Chambers

In looking back to former days, I recollect with pride the friendship which existed between Chambers and myself. I owe my presence at the battle of Waterloo to him; for by him I was introduced to Sir Thomas Picton, and it was by his advice that I joined my regiment the day before the battle. After Picton's death, poor Chambers, in carrying orders to Sir James Kempt to retake at all hazards the farm of La Haye Sainte, advanced at the head of the attacking column, and was in the act of receiving the sword of a French officer who had surrendered to him, when he received a musket ball through the lungs, which killed him on the spot. When the Duke of York heard of his death, H.R.H. exclaimed, "In him we have lost one of our most promising officers."

Captain Robert Adair, of the 1st Guards

No language can express the admiration felt by all who witnessed the heroic exploits of poor Adair. During the charges of the French cavalry, which were always preceded by a tremendous fire of artillery at point-blank distance, we lost many men. The cuirassiers and heavy dragoons approached so close, that it was feared they would enter by the gap which had been made in our square. Adair rushed forward, placed himself in the open space, and with one blow of his sword killed a French officer who had actually got amongst our men. After many exploits, showing a coolness and a courage rarely equalled, and never surpassed, Adair was struck towards the end of the day by a cannon ball, which shattered his thigh near the hip. His sufferings during the amputation were dreadful; the shot had torn away the flesh of the thigh, and the bones were sticking up near the hip in splinters. The surgeon, Mr Gilder, had much difficulty in using his knife, having blunted it, and all his other instruments, by amputations in the earlier part of the battle. Poor Adair during the operation had sufficient pluck to make one last ghastly joke, saying, "Take your time, Mr Carver." He soon afterwards died from loss of blood.

ENSIGN SOMERVILLE BUEGES, OF THE 1ST FOOT GUARDS

He enjoyed soldiering in the real sense of the word, and sought glory on every field of battle. He entered the Guards before he attained the age of seventeen, and his buoyant spirits and athletic frame fitted him for a military life. I breakfasted with him on the morning of the battle. After many acts of great personal courage he was wounded by a cannon ball which shattered his leg in a frightful manner. Amputation was the consequence; and after the surgeon had dressed the wounds, he hailed some soldiers to carry Burges to the cart, upon which the latter declined being carried, saying, " I will hop into it;" and he succeeded in performing this extraordinary feat without further injury to the wounded stump. This heroic soldier, owing to the regulations then in force, was put on the shelf for the remainder of his life.

CAPTAIN PERCIVAL, OF THE 1ST GUARDS

The wound which Captain Percival received was one of the most painful it ever fell to a soldier's lot to bear. He received a ball which carried away all his teeth and both his jaws, and left nothing on the mouth but the skin of the cheeks. Percival recovered sufficiently to join our regiment in the Tower, three years subsequent to the battle of Waterloo. He had to be fed with porridge and a few spoonfuls of broth; but notwithstanding all the care to preserve his life, he sunk from inanition and died very shortly after, his body presenting the appearance of a skeleton.

CAPTAIN CURZON

Among the many episodes of a battle-field, there is none so touching as the last moments of a brave soldier. Captain Curzon, son of Lord Scarsdale, was on the staff, and received a mortal wound towards the end of the battle, and lay bleeding to death by the side of his favourite charger, one of whose legs had been shattered by a cannon ball. As Lord March was passing by, Curzon had just strength to call to him, "Get me help, my dear March, for I fear it is all over with me."

Lord March hastened to look for a surgeon, and found one belonging to the first battalion of our regiment, who went to the poor fellow's assistance; but alas! life was extinct before the doctor arrived. The doctor, in relating this event to us afterwards, said, "I found poor Curzon dead, leaning his head upon the neck of his favourite horse, which seemed to be aware of the death of his master, so quiet did it remain, as if afraid to disturb his last sleep. As I approached, it neighed feebly, and looked at me as if it wanted relief from the pain of its shattered limb, so I told a soldier to shoot it through the head to put it out of its pain. The horse as well as its master were both old acquaintances of mine, and I was quite upset by the sight of them lying dead together."

This tribute of sympathy and feeling was the more remarkable as coming from the doctor, who was one of the hardest and roughest diamonds I ever remember to have known; but on this occasion something moved him, and he had tears in his eyes as he related the incident.

CAPTAIN KELLY, OF THE LIFE GUARDS

This chivalrous man, of undaunted courage and very powerful frame, in the deadly encounter with the cuirassiers of the Imperial Guard, performed prodigies of valour.

In the gallant and, for a time, successful charge of the Household Brigade, he greatly distinguished himself; and when our gallant fellows, after sustaining a terrible fire of artillery, were attacked by an overwhelming force of French cavalry, and were forced to retreat behind our squares, Kelly was seen cutting his way through a host of enemies. Shaw, the famous prize-fighter, a private in his regiment, came to his assistance, and these two heroes fought side by side, killing or disabling many of their antagonists, till poor Shaw, after receiving several wounds, was killed from a thrust through the body by a French colonel of *cuirassiers*, who in his turn received a blow from Kelly's sword, which cut through his helmet and stretched him lifeless upon the ground.

I recollect questioning my friend Kelly about this celebrated charge, at our mess at Windsor in 1816, when he said that he owed his life to the excellence of his charger, which was well bred, very well broke, and of immense power. He thought that with an ordinary horse he would have been killed a hundred times in the numerous encounters which he had to sustain.

A French Officer's Account

Anonymous

A French Officer's Account

The army of the North, on its arrival at Beaumont, jointed that of the Ardennes, commanded by Vandamme, whose head-quarters were at Furnay. The army of the Moselle, under General Girard, quitting Metz by forced marches, debouched in the same period by Philippeville, and brought itself likewise into line. Thus the army of the North consisted of five corps of infantry, under the command of the Lieutenant-generals D'Erlon, Reille, Vandamme, Girard, and the Count de Lobau. The cavalry, commanded in chief by Marshal Grouchy, was divided into four corps, under the orders of Generals Pajol, Excelmans, Milhaud, and Kellerman.

The imperial guard, which was composed of twenty thousand men, formed the nucleus of this fine army, which was followed by a considerable *materiel* of artillery, perfectly well equipped, and in the best possible condition, as well as a great many pontoons. Beside the battering-train attached to each division, every corps of the army had its park of reserve. The guards, in particular, had a magnificent artillery, almost wholly composed of new pieces.

These chosen troops, might amount to about one hundred and fifty thousand effective men, of which twenty thousand were cavalry, accompanied with three hundred pieces of ordnance. But, already in the interior of their own country, the troops evinced a want of discipline, which constitutes the strength of armies, and the security of the countries to which they belong.

Regardless of their unhappy countrymen, who manifested the greatest zeal in furnishing every kind of subsistence in their power, the French soldiers treated them with the most cruel rigour, and considered plunder as one of their most incontestable privileges, and made a sort of merit in giving themselves up to every species of excess.

Every where they sacked the houses; and, under pretext of searching for provisions, burst open the doors, broke open the closets, ill-treated the peasants, and seized upon whatever they chose. 'They had taken the field,' they said, 'and the war could not be carried on without them;' consequently every thing was allowed them, and they gave a full scope to their taste for plunder—a taste which can only be compared, for the ravages committed during a ten year's war, to the excursions of barbarous hordes upon the lands of their neighbours. In this manner, roaming from house to house, from granary to granary, from one cellar to another, the soldiers returned to their camp loaded with plunder, after having barbarously destroyed what they could not carry away. The peasant considered himself unusually fortunate, if, after enduring all sorts of abuse and ill-treatment, he escaped their vengeance, by leaving his all to their discretion.

To this infamous pillage, the greater part of the officers opposed by a feeble resistance; nay, they even tolerated it, under the ready excuse, 'We must not be too severe: the soldier must live.' And, whilst the soldier has his subsistence, it may be easily conceived the officer had an abundance, and was only perplexed by the difficulty of choice.

Do we recognise here, it may be asked, the frank and loyal character of the French officer? Certainly not. But let not the French name be disgraced in the estimation of posterity, because the officers of Buonaparte were not those of Turenne and Villeroi. In the midst of this herd of lawless and unprincipled devastators, there were not wanting many men of honour and principle, who lamented over this frightful disorder, and who served with profound regret in this rebellious army, but who endeavoured to persuade themselves that it was their duty to defend their country under any leader. A principle of military honour kept them firm to their post. They were indifferent to Napoleon, but they were attached to France.

Nor was it, perhaps, possible to repress those disorders in an army which had been formed to them by the habit and example of twenty years. It was, in fact, by this system of brigandage, that Napoleon had succeeded in so firmly attaching the soldiers to his name and cause.

The country which the troops were traversing, covered with wheat already browning, promised a luxuriant harvest: but this abundance existed in vain; woe to the fields through which was the passage of the army; and still more so to those which became the position of a camp. In a few moments, the labour and gift of the year were trodden under foot by men and horses, or torn up by the roots for fodder.

The interior of the army was distracted by intestine divisions and anarchy. It seems as if the different corps were animated with a hatred of each other, and that open war existed between them. Above all, there was no agreement between the chiefs.

When a commandant of a column, or a regiment, arrived at the place which it was to occupy, he seized upon whatever was found there, without any regard to who might come after him. A guard was placed upon those houses which furnished any supplies, and, without any other right than that of being the first occupied, every share was denied. Frequently, indeed, they fell upon the sentries, and a disgraceful conflict ensued. In this manner a number of men were wounded, and some were actually killed.

The *imperial guard* conducted themselves with great arrogance towards the other troops, and were particularly hated by them; and, for the disdain which they showed towards others, they were themselves persecuted in their turn, whenever they were not strong enough to give the law.

The cavalry, in like manner, insulted the infantry with every kind of outrage; and the infantry menaced the cavalry with their bayonets, and affected to despise them. Such was the condition of the army which was marched upon the frontiers to protect and defend the citizens: they had put them in a condition not to dread the presence of a most ferocious enemy.

In this state they proceeded by forced marches: the weather, although constantly showery, had nevertheless been tolerably fine, so that the roads did not impede the march of the artillery and carriages. The movements were effected with a celerity bordering upon precipitation. It was evidently the intention to surprise the enemy by an unexpected appearance, and these rapid marches rendered a sudden irruption into Belgium highly probable.

On the 14th the whole army was found united in line upon the extreme frontier; and the uncertainty which had hitherto subsisted respecting the intention of the manoeuvres, caused the publication of a proclamation, which was inserted in the order of the day, and read at the head of each regiment.

This proclamation was received with transports of joy and loud acclamations by the multitude of ignorant soldiers, to whom a few high-sounding words which they do not understand, seem the very height of eloquence. The proclamation itself wears the same stamp with all the other productions of Napoleon, and only differs from them in greater extravagance and absurdity. Whoever weighed the incoherent declamation of that vain-glorious prophet, looked on it with pity. Meanwhile it increased the public unrest by laying open the whole extent of the dangers which Buonaparte intended to brave. The chiefs, however, were delighted with the precision of their routes, and recognised the presence of the great man in those scientific combinations, by which all the masses of the army, after encumbering each other's march, seemed all at once to rise from the ground, and find themselves ranged in line by the effect of magic. Such is the power of prepossession.

On the 15th, at break of day, this army broke up for the Belgic territory. The second division attacked the Prussian outposts, and pursued them as far as Marchienne-au-Pont; the cavalry of this body had to charge several corps of infantry different times, which they drove back, took some hundreds of prisoners, and the Prussians were obliged to re-cross the Sambre. The light cavalry of the centre followed the second division on the road to Charleroi, and, chasing away in different charges such of the enemy as they met, drove the whole to the other side. While numerous sharp-shooters defended the approach to the bridge, the Prussians were employed in rendering it impassable, in order to retard our march, and afford them time to evacuate the city, but being too closely pushed, they were unable to destroy it effectually, and our men soon removed all difficulties to their passage over it. About noon their work was completed, and the light cavalry took possession of Charleroi.

The second corps, in the mean time, having effected a passage lower down the river at Marchienne, advanced upon Gosselies, a large town upon the opposite side of the river, and through which was a road to Brussels. The object of this movement was to prevent the Prussians from retiring upon this point, when they should be driven from Charleroi by the attack which was then proceeding. The Prussians, thus forced in front, and anticipated upon our flank, retired upon Fleurus, where they began to occupy themselves in concentrating their army.

Whilst the Prussians were employed in this operation, they had to sustain themselves against the repeated attacks of our divisions, who unceasingly interrupted them whilst taking their position.

The presence of Buonaparte so electrified the French troops, that the divisions, as fast as they arrived, threw themselves upon the enemy with such irresistible impetuosity, as to bear down every thing before them. They scarcely discharged a musket, but, with fixed bayonets, dashed into the thickest of the enemy's masses.

The squadrons of Napoleon's body-guard made several charges upon the Prussian infantry; in one of which, General Letort, Colonel of the dragoons of the guard, received a mortal wound. The French finally succeeded in driving the enemy from all his positions on the Sambre.

Towards night the combat ceased; and Buonaparte, after having left the third corps on its route towards Namur, and the second at Gosselies upon the road to Brussels, returned to Charleroi as his head-quarters. The remainder of the army occupied the surrounding villages. The results of these different engagements were a thousand prisoners, the passage of the Sambre; and the possession of Charleroi and its magazines.

But it was a still more signal advantage, that it confirmed the courage of the troops by success. Napoleon availed himself of this success, and of its fruits, according to his usual system.

The prisoners were paraded with the artifice of a procession at a theatre, by the effect of which a few bands, carefully repeated, and systematically re-introduced, appear to be an army. Thus the prisoners were marched in presence of different divisions from the front to the rear. The air resounded with the cries of *Vive l'Empereur!* and the soldiers believed every thing done in this auspicious commencement of the campaign. In the beginning of this day, the Prussian army, consisting of four corps, were encamped on the line of the Sambre; they fell back to the points of concentration, Fleurus, Namur, Cincy, and Hannut. The principal corps engaged with us was that of General Zeithen. This general was at Fleurus, where he received us bravely.

Blucher was informed of these events in the course of the afternoon, and immediately ordered his other three corps (those at Namur, Cincy, and Hannut) to advanced by a forced march to Sombref, about four miles from Fleurus, where he intended to put himself at their head, and give us battle on the following day.

The whole of the French army was now in the territory of Belgium, in the midst of the new subjects of the kingdom of the Netherlands, who welcomed up with acclamations, as their deliverers, and asserted that they only waited for our arrival to rise en masse in favour of our cause.

We found, in fact, a few groups of peasants at the entrance of the villages we passed through, who came to meet us with cries of *Vive l'Empereur!* they did not appear however to be animated by a sincere enthusiasm; and, to speak frankly, they rather resembled hired criers, than citizens, who were anxious to express their real sentiments.

They received us as conquerors, whose good-will it was necessary to conciliate; or rather, they were friends of the strongest party, and their exclamations evidently meant thus: 'We are willing to be French subjects, if your bayonets give the law. Do not plunder us, do not ravage our fields; but treat us as your countrymen.'

These supplications, however, were disregarded; and notwithstanding the confidence our soldiers gave to these friendly demonstrations, they treated them as their most decided enemies: devastation and rapine every where marked the march of the army. No sooner had the troops taken up a temporary position in the neighbourhood of some village, than they rushed like a torrent upon the ill-fated houses; provisions, drink, furniture, and clothes, all disappeared in an instant. A village near which they had encamped, when they quitted in the next morning, presented only a vast heap of ruins, around which lay dispersed, all that had served as the furniture of the houses.

The surrounding country, which was for the most part covered with corn, seemed to have been destroyed by a hailstorm; and the places where the bivouac-fires had been made, remained black, and, scattered over the meadows and corn-fields, now reduced to stubble, appeared like places struck with lightning.

The instant the troops departed, the inhabitants, over-whelmed with terror, the women dissolved in tears, the children half naked and seized with horror, emerged in swarms from the hiding-places, and ran over their devastated fields, to recognise the various utensils which constituted their property, and to collect the wreck.

We now learned, that the Prussian out-posts, although on their guard, were surprised; and that, far from expecting an aggression so hasty and so serious, the allies were intending, in the course of a few days, to enter the French territory.

The inhabitants themselves were thunder-struck at our appearance, at a time when they thought us employed in securing our own frontiers from invasion. They spoke very ill of the Prussians, who they represented as very extortionate, and who daily ill-treated them.

From these reports, which conveyed no positive information, every one formed his own opinion upon the probable result of the campaign. The general idea was, that the allied army not being united, could not effect its concentration; that the divided corps, sharply pursued, and turned on every side, would make but a feeble defence. That Lord Wellington would be to tally disconcerted by this unexpected movement, and that all his plans for the campaign would be rendered abortive.

Besides this, the troops had such entire confidence in Buonaparte, whose combinations were considered as certain as they were admirable, that nothing was now thought of but the destruction of the English, or a precipitate embarkation, a speedy arrival upon the Rhine, amidst the shouts of the Belgians, risen in mass, and eager for the opportunity of rejoining their old companions in arms.

At three o'clock, on the morning of the 16th, the columns which remained on the right bank of the Sambre, put themselves in motion, and passed the river, when the whole army advanced forward. The command of the left wing, consisting of the first and second divisions of infantry, and four corps of cavalry, was given to Marshal Ney, who had arrived the preceding evening at head-quarters, and received orders to march by Gossilies and Frasnes on the road to Brussels.

The centre, composed of the third, fourth, and sixth divisions, the reserve, and a numerous body of cavalry, forming the mass of the army, directed itself upon Fleurus. Marshal Grouchy, with the cavalry of Pajol, and some battalions of foot, manoeuvred towards the village of Sombref, on the road to Namur.

They soon discovered the Prussian army; the chief masses of which appeared in close columns, crowning the upland levels that surround the mill of Bussi, and stretching in amphitheatre through the whole length of a sloping hill, in front of which was a deep ravine.

In the mean time, the fourth corps precipitated itself with great alacrity upon Ligny, and a desperate conflict was commenced upon this point. Each party fought with the greatest obstinacy, and for a long time there appeared no thought of yielding on either side.

At the same moment, our two wings had come to the engagement with the opposite wings of the enemy; our right, directing itself against the enemy at Sombref, whilst our left advanced against Frasnes.

Every part of both armies (with the exception of our reserve) was thus engaged; the affair therefore was now general, and the cannonade, increasing every instant, roared in tremendous horror along the lines.

The combat was kept up on both sides with equal obstinacy. It is impossible to form an idea of the fury which animated the soldiers of the two parties against each other; it seemed as if each of them had a personal injury to revenge, and had found in his adversary his most implacable enemy. The French would give no quarter; the Prussians, they said, had vowed to massacre all the French that should fall into their hands: these menaces were particularly addressed to the guard, against whom they appeared to have an uncommon spite. In fact, on both sides the carnage was awful in the extreme.

The villages which formed the theatre of action were taken and retaken several times with a horrible loss of life. At last the French confronted the allies and particularlythe British at Quatre Bras.

Along the whole front a hollow road, which had the appearance of a ravine, and plains covered with rye of a tolerable size separated this road from the wood, the right of which was occupied by the French, to a certain extent. In a moment these plains were covered with numerous battalions formed in squares, supported by a formidable cavalry, who advanced with great confidence, and threatened to force our line. Our troops appeared intimidated, and recoiled with a sort of panic.

The moment was very pressing, and it was necessary to hasten the reserves. Marshal Ney, however, who was little alarmed at these attempts, as he relied on the first corps, sent an order for them to march instantly to the spot, and to charge the enemy. But what was his astonishment and confusion, when he found that Buonaparte had otherwise disposed of them!

He immediately ordered the eighth and the eleventh cuirassiers, who happened to be at hand, to charge the first battalions. This charge was executed with the greatest resolution; but these battalions, being supported from behind with the infantry which filled the wood, were enabled to open such a terrible fire upon us, that our cuirassiers, being repelled in their attempt to pierce the, were obliged to make a wheel round; and, as always happens in such cases, retired in much disorder.

Such was the effect of Napoleon's withdrawing the first corps from Marshal Ney. And the first corps was as useless to the emperor, as it would have been effectual to Marshal Ney; as it was merely employed in marching and returning.

In the meantime the fire continued with increased vivacity along the whole line, and particularly towards Ligny, where the greater part of both armies were assembled, and upon which, therefore, each directed its principal efforts. The cannonade, indeed, never relaxed for an instant; and our artillery, as far as I could form a judgment from what I saw, made a most dreadful havoc in the Prussian columns, which, being posted in masses on the opposite ridge of hills, and upon *plateaux* just below our batteries and position, afforded us a point-blank aim at less than half-cannon shot.

Our own troops, on the other hand, carefully posted in the sinuosities of the ground, and at the foot of the hills, were, comparatively, little exposed to the Prussian artillery; which thus made more noise than effect, and reminded every military man of the ferocious whiskers and cowardly hearts,—the warlike dress, and insignificant minds, of the Prussian officers.

About seven in the evening, we were masters of the field. At Ligny, the most obstinate defence, the Prussians were driven back, and left us masters of the field of battle, covered with the dead, the dying, the wounded, some prisoners, and a few field-pieces. The guards immediately possessed themselves of the slopes and uplands which were evacuated, and our cavalry pursued the fugitives. During this decisive operation at Ligny, the third corps were endeavouring to employ the Prussian right wing, in order to divert their attention from what had passed. But they readily saw through our design, and effected their retreat to Gembloux and Namur.

The French army prepared to push their success; but the approach of night, and the fatigues of the day, prevented it. They contented themselves, therefore, with taking possession of all the Prussian posts, and at ten o'clock, the fire had ceased along the whole line.

A variety of extravagant reports were circulated in our army respecting the battle. Marshal Blucher had, in fact, a horse killed under him; he was stunned by the fall, and sur-rounded by French cuirassiers; it was to the darkness of the night alone he owed his safety. But, notwithstanding, the Prus-sians must have severely suffered; their loss was never known, nor even attended to in our orders. On the left, where the English were engaged, both parties maintained their ground and their positions.

The death of the Duke of Brunswick was announced, killed from the fire of the division commanded by Jerome Buonaparte; and also of General Hill. The first intelligence was confirmed the following day, and urged our French gen-erals to interweave, for the purpose of currying favour with the ex-king of Westphalia, some unbecoming pleasantries on the fatality that seemed to pursue the unfortunate duke, who, placed in constant opposition with the conqueror of his states, was condemned to die by his hand. And the latter, they augured hence, was again called to be his successor. It was added, that Jerome himself had been struck by a spent bullet. We will not stop to examine the truth of a fact of so trivial importance: but it is observable that this sort of shot never reaches any but great personages, whose valour it is in-teresting to enhance. Every one agreed that Buonaparte had obtained his end in separating the Prussians and the English; and that, having so much weakened the former, he had now only to encounter the latter.

It was to realize the hope of exterminating the English, that, on the 17th, at day-break, Buonaparte, leaving behind him the third and fourth corps, together with the cavalry of General Pajol, under command of Marshal Grouchy, to watch the Prussians, marched with his reserve, and the sixth corps, towards Quatre Bras.

The English appeared to occupy the same positions as on the day preceding; and the French army remained till eleven o'clock in the forenoon, observing them, and waiting for the troops from the right, whose arrival was delayed by heavy rains and cross-roads almost impracticable.

Arrangements were made for the attack, and the units corps advanced in front of battle, along the heights of Frasnes, when it was perceived that the English had manoeuvred so as to mask their retreat. The troops we saw on the plain, at the entrance of the wood, and on the road, were only a strong rear-guard to cover the same. Buonaparte set out in pursuit of them with his cavalry, and all the army urged its march to Brussels.

During this rapid march, the ardour of the troops was in-credible; they saw only in the expert and well-regulated re-treat of the English, a total rout, which must terminate by their embarkation. Already they were promising themselves that they would no more make a stand, but that, giving up to their own resources, they would push on, abandoning Brussels to us, and regain their vessels with all possible expedition.

The artillery, infantry, and carriages, filed along with great embarrassment and precipitation in the high road, covered with a thick mud, while the cavalry marched by the sides, across corn-fields, which were every where very beautiful, and which they reduced to manure.

The horses plunged up to the belly into this black soil, which was softened and extremely adhesive, and could not be detached without great difficulty; which materially retarded the march, and rendered it extremely painful. On the road

were found several English *caissons*, which had been abandoned, and carriages with broken wheels.

We passed over the field of battle of Quatre Bras, which
was covered with dead bodies, and with wrecks, on which
was also found a tolerable number of wounded French who
had not been carried off. We could here judge how destructive the affair had been to both parties; but, according to ap-
pearances, the loss of the English had been much greater than
ours. The plains, which separated the wood where they were
posted, from the high road, and particularly the borders of this
wood and the hollow road before mentioned, were concealed
from view by heaps of dead bodies, the greatest part of which
were Scotch. Their costume, particularly attracted the attention of the French soldiers, who called them *sans-culottes*.

Buonaparte, with his advanced-guard, pursued the English
till night, and did not halt till he arrived at the forest of Soignies, where they opposed to him a resistance which he de-
spaired of overcoming that day. After cannonading, and har-
assing them, as long as the day-light permitted him, he caused
his troops to take up a position, and fixed his head-quarters at
the farm of Caillou, near Planchenoit.

The principal masses of the army encamped at Gemappe,
and in the neighbourhood of that small town. The night was
tremendous; a continual rain, which fell in torrents, made the
troops suffer cruelly, who were bivouacked in the midst of
the mud, and wet corn-fields, and had not time to construct
themselves shelter. But if this night was terrible to the soldiers, how much worse was it to the unfortunate inhabitants
of the country, who, overwhelmed with terror, had quitted
their houses, which were given up to all kinds of rapine.

It was generally supposed that the English would avail
themselves of the night to continue their retreat, and no one
had the least doubt but we should arrive at Brussels the next
day; thus they amused themselves with considering the cam-

paign as at an end, as they already believed themselves masters of that town, and that Marshal Grouchy, who they supposed would halt that night at Namur, could not fail to arrive at Liege, at the same time that Buonaparte entered the capital of the Netherlands.

Some *soi-disant* deserters, who were no better than spies, assured us that the Belgian army was only waiting for an engagement to come over in a body to our side, but that, as their inclinations were known, they had been always kept in the rear, since the commencement of hostilities; it was, nevertheless, believed they would unexpectedly rise upon the Prussians, against whom they had a mortal antipathy.

Our first surprise, as the day dawned, was to see that the English, instead of retiring, had resumed their position, and seemed resolved to defend it. Buonaparte, who had no apprehension during the night, but that they would escape the punishment which he designed for them, was animated with a most sensible joy, at seeing them at their post; he was too fond of the game of war, and thought that he played it too well to have any pleasure in a game only abandoned to him. He could not retain the expression of his feeling to those around him.—"Bravo!" said he, "the English!—Ah! I have them, then,—these English."

He now hastened up, with all that imprudent impatience which characterizes him, the march of all the columns in the rear; and, without any other information than what his eye afforded him,—without knowing either the position or the forces of his enemy,—without ascertaining that the Prussian army was held in check by Marshal Grouchy, he resolved to attack them on the spot.

The French army, which consisted of four corps of infantry, including the guard, and of three corps of cavalry, formed an effective force of one hundred and twenty thousand men. About ten in the morning of this day (the 18th of June,) the whole of this force was assembled in advance of Planchenois. The position was upon two eminences, parallel to two opposite ranges occupied by the English army, the English having taken their position upon some *plateaux* situated in advance of the forest of Soignies.

Towards the centre of the line, which was upon Mont St. Jean, in the rear of the mount, and, around the farm of the same name, we perceived some strong and deep masses of infantry: they crowned a vast *plateau* or platform of ground, which extended itself on both sides of the forest; but the line, to appearance, at least, diminished in depth as it extended, and was covered with batteries.

The right of the English army extended itself upon the village of Merke Brain, having in front of it the farm of Hougoumont, surrounded with intersected ravines; their left was extended towards Wavre, and was covered in front by a ravine and the farm of La Haye Sainte.

We could not follow this line with our eyes through its whole extent; but it appeared to terminate behind the village of Smouhen, where was the position of the Brunswick troops. Generally speaking, with the exception of the great *plateaux* in and about Mont St. Jean, which formed the centre of the English line, we saw but a few troops; but naturally supposed that they were stationed, and thereby concealed, in the gorges which separated the flats from the forest, and the forest itself.

The head-quarters of the Duke of Wellington were at Waterloo, in the rear of all his lines; and the lines were so established as to intersect and to cover the roads of Brussels and Nivelles.

Scarcely had the French troops all assembled, when Buonaparte, who was stationed on a hillock, situated at a very short distance from the place where he had slept, on the right of the road, near the far of La Belle Alliance, whence he could discover all the movements, sent an order to commence the action: he was walking alone, with his arms crossed upon his breast, in front, and at a short distance from his staff, who were ranged in a line behind him. The day was stormy; and there fell, at intervals, a few showers, which were not of long continuance. This weather continued during the day.

The second corps was placed on the left, and marched against the farm of Hougoumont. The first rested its left upon the high road, and extended towards the centre. The sixth occupied the right. The guard remained in reserve upon the heights. The cavalry was divided between the different points, but the strongest columns of those troops occupied the two wings, and particularly the right.

Towards noon, the first discharge of cannon resounded from the French lines, and numerous riflemen detached themselves in order to commence the action. The left attacked the farm of Hougoumont, the buildings of which had been looped by the infantry, who occupied them in great force, and who fought with extreme obstinacy. The battalions and squadrons marched against the masses stationed behind this far, and who sent continually reinforcements to it.

The engagement soon grew serious upon the right; and the centre, advancing gradually to follow the movement of the two wings, and to act in concert with them, an extremely heavy firing was opened along the whole of the line; the affair was become general, and promised, from the commencement, to be very hot and serious.

After an hour's murderous conflict, during which the artillery and musketry of both sides were served in the most gallant style, the English appeared to retire a little, and the French army pressed its approaches: the artillery advanced in front throughout the whole line, and the columns followed it.

Our troops were thus all engaged by degrees, not without suffering great losses, amidst the difficulties of an uneven

ground, hilly, and intersected by hollows, deep ditches, and ravines, where they were stopped at every step by fresh masses,
which, being concealed by the ground, were not perceived till
they fell upon them.

Every foot of ground was disputed, and only yielded, on
either side, when all means of resistance were exhausted; the
smallest hillocks, the most inconsiderate hollows, were often
taken and retaken several times. Repeated charges of cavalry
were carried into execution; the field of battle was heaped
with dead bodies; and the firing, instead of relaxing in the
least, was increasing continually in violence.

The combat was sustained on both sides with equal fury;
the defence was as obstinate as the attack was impetuous.
In a short time it was announced, that very strong columns
were marching, the bayonet in front, upon Mont St. Jean, at
the same time that the cavalry of the wings were to charge
the batteries, which appeared to be but little protected. This
grand movement, from the result of which so much might be
expected, was impatiently waited for; but the obstinate perseverance of the English in maintaining their position in the
villages which flanked their wings, retarded it.

They successively sent battalions towards the farms of
Hougoumont and La Haye Sainte, which were as frequently
driven back by our cavalry; yet those villages, though pressed
with unparalleled vigour, still defended themselves. Eager to
drive the enemy from Hougoumont, who appeared resolved
not to retire, we determined to set fire to it, at the same time
sending a reinforcement against La Haye Sainte, which we
carried after a most sanguinary contest.

The English artillery made dreadful havoc in our ranks: we
were so completely exposed, that their rockets passed easily
through all our lines, and fell in the midst of our equipage,
which was placed behind on the road, and its environs. A
number of shells also burst amongst them, and rendered it

indispensable for the train to retire to a greater distance. This was not effected without considerable disorder, which was clearly perceived by the English.

Our artillery re-opened their fire with equal vivacity; but probably with much less effect, as their masses could only be levelled against by approximation, being almost entirely masked by the inequalities of the ground. The unremitting thunder of more than six hundred pieces of artillery; the fire of the battalions and light troops; the frequent explosion of caissons, blown up by shells which reached them; the hissing of balls and grape-shot; the clash of arms; the tumultuous roar of the charges, and shouts of a soldiery— all created an effect of sound, which the pen would in vain attempt to describe; and all this within a narrow space, the two armies being close to each other, and their respective lines contracted into the shortest possible length. However, in spite of obstacles and dangers, the French army was sensibly gaining ground.

The support of the two British wings being carried, we passed the ravine, and advanced amidst a deluge of balls and grape-shot. A strong column approached Mont St. Jean, whence a terrific fire was pouring. The French cavalry, at the same time, rushed to carry the guns on the plains, but was charged in its turn by the enemy's horse, who issued in a body from the hollows where they had lain in ambuscade, and the slaughter became terrible. Neither side receded one step; fresh columns reinforced them; the charge was repeated. Three times the French were on the point of forcing the positions, and three times they were driven back.

These assaults, made without interruption, and with all the impetuosity which distinguishes the French, caused the enemy considerable loss, and obliged him to make the greatest efforts of resistance. Lord Wellington exposed himself considerably; and, in order to be able to direct all his means in person, threw himself frequently into the midst of the conflict, to show himself to his soldiers, and inspire them with confidence by his presence. The Prince of Orange, who was in the right wing, was wounded at the head of his troops.

If, however, witnesses, worthy of credit, may be believed, the English were very near being forced. It has also been confidently asserted, that the greatest disorder prevailed in their rear for some time, and that their carriages were made to retrograde precipitately, which file on the Brussels road with great confusion, amidst a general panic.

But, be that as it will, it is not less certain, that they repulsed, with an insurmountable firmness, all our attempts, and succeeded in rendering them fruitless, by concealing from our observation the derangement and fears, which such furious attacks, so often and so obstinately repeated, certainly inspired.

At the same instant as they began to be sensibly alarmed, there was also in the French army a hesitation and evident uneasiness; some battalions that had been overthrown retreated; great numbers of wounded detached themselves from the columns, and spread ideas of the greatest uncertainty respecting the issues of the battle; and a profound silence had succeeded to acclamations of the soldiers, who had made sure of victory.

With the exception of the infantry of the guard, the whole of the troops were seen to be exposed to the most murderous fire; the action was still kept up with the same violence, but without any important result.

It was now near seven o'clock: Buonaparte, who hitherto had remained where he was first stationed, and whence he could see all that passed, was contemplating, with a ferocious aspect, the hideous spectacle of such a horrid butchery. The more the difficulties increased, the more obstinate he was. He became angry at these unforeseen obstacles; and, far from fearing to push too far the trial of any army, whose confidence in him was unbounded, he continued to send fresh troops, and to give the orders to advance, to *charge bayonet*, to *carry* every thing. Several times he was informed that different points of the army were in a perilous situation; and that the troops appeared to give up: but his only answer was—*Forward! forward!*

One general sent him intelligence, that he was in a position which could not be kept, being mowed down by a battery. He asked of him, at the same time, what he should do to withdraw himself from the destructive fire of this battery. *Storm it!* he replied, and turned his back on the aide-de-camp.

A British officer, who was wounded, and a prisoner, was brought before him. He endeavoured to obtain some information from him, and asked, among other things, what was the force of the English army? The officer told him that it was very numerous, and that it had just received a reinforcement of sixty thousand men. 'So much the better,' he said; 'the more there are, the more we shall beat.' He sent off several *estafettes* with despatches, which he dictated to a secretary, and repeated several times, 'See that he does not forget to say every where that the victory is mine.'

It was at this epoch, and at the moment when all his enterprises had completely miscarried, that it was announced to him, that some Prussian columns had appeared on our right flank, and were menacing our rear; but he would not give any credit to this report, and replied several times, that these pretended Prussians were nothing else than the corps of Grouchy. He even sent back with ill-humour several of his aides-de-camp, who successively brought him these tidings. 'Go along,' said he, 'you have been frightened; approach without fear to the columns which have appeared, and you will be convinced that they are those of Grouchy.

After so positive an answer, several of them, in confusion for their mistake, returned with confidence towards the Prussians advanced corps, and, notwithstanding the warm fire which these directed against them, approached so near as to run the risk of being killed or made prisoners.

It was necessary, therefore, to yield to evidence, and it was, besides, impossible any longer to mistake the truth of what was stated, when these columns, filing off as they arrived, made a fierce attack on our right. Part of the sixth corps was sent to support this new shock, in expectation of the arrival of Marshal Grouchy's divisions, which were continually anticipated; the report was even spread in the army that they were already in line.

It results from the accounts, that part of Marshal Blucher's army, which, after the battle of the 16th, had carefully concentrated itself near Wavre, had concealed its march from Marshal Grouchy; and that after being rejoined by the fourth Prussian corps under General Bulow, had with great expedition re-approached the English line, to co-operate with the Duke of Wellington.

Marshal Grouchy had, in fact, pursued the Prussians closely in their retreat upon Wavre, and had in that place attacked the portion of their army which remained there. He was fighting, at the very time that we were also engaged, against some small corps, which he mistook for the whole of the Prussian army, over which he continued to gain signal advantages.

These corps, however, being favoured by the difficulties of a mountainous country, opposed him with a resistance obstinate enough, if not to arrest his march, at least to retard it considerably. They thus succeeded in engaging him at a sufficient distance from the place where the business was really to be decided, and thus prevented his having any share in that decision. For this reason he was of no assistance to us; and thus the English received a considerable reinforcement, whose intervention, which they well knew how to value, and which was also foreseen, enabled them not only to be fearless of our most vigorous attempts, but to resume against us the offensive, and shortly to overpower us. They therefore re-assumed an entire confidence; and, calculating their dispositions from the favourable circumstances which presented themselves, they resisted with all their strength, and with an ardour incessantly renewed.

It is, besides, evident, that this operation had been concerted between the two commanders-in-chief, and that the English defended their position with a steadiness so insuperable, only to give time to the Prussians for effecting this combined movement; on which depended the success of the battle, the commencement of which they hourly expected.

Buonaparte, who, in despite of all, appeared to have no doubt concerning the speedy arrival of Marshal Grouchy, and who, undoubtedly, persuaded himself that he pressed closely on the Prussian army, judged with a determination which nothing could alter, that the moment for deciding the day was arrived. He accordingly formed a fourth column of attack, composed almost entirely of the guard, and, after sending off to every point instructions for supporting this movement on which the victory depended, directed it at the *pas de charge* on Mont St. Jean.

These old warriors rushed upon the plain with the intrepidity one might expect from them: the whole army resumed its vigour, the fire was again lighted up along the line, the guard made several charges, but their efforts were constantly repulsed; being destroyed by a formidable artillery which appeared to multiply.

These invincible grenadiers beheld their ranks shattered by the grape-shot; they closed them, however, with great coolness, still marching on without being intimidated; nothing arrested their progress, but death or serious wounds; but the hour of defeat was come; enormous masses of infantry, supported by an immense cavalry, to which we could no longer oppose any, our own being entirely destroyed, poured upon them with fury, and, surrounding them on all sides, summoned them to surrender: *'The guard never surrender—they die,'* was their answer. From that time no more quarter was given them, almost the whole fell, fighting like desperadoes, beneath the strokes of sabres, or of bayonets: this horrible massacre continued as long as their resistance, but, at length, overpowered by forces vastly superior, and discouraged besides, from opposing themselves in vain to certain destruction, they quitted their ranks, and fell back in disorder to their first positions, with the design, no doubt, of there rallying again.

During these events in the centre, the Prussian columns having arrived on our right, continued to advance, and to press with ardour the few troops that were found on that point; a cannonading and a brisk fire of musketry were heard in the rear of our line, and approached nearer and nearer; our troops sustained the combat as long as possible, but they gradually lost ground. At last our right wing retrograded sensibly, and the Prussians, who were turning it, were on the point of bursting on the high road, when the report was circulated that the guard had been repulsed, anal that its battalions, scattered and reduced to a small number, were seen to retire with precipitation. A general panic now spread itself throughout the army, who dispersed in all directions, and sought their safety in the most precipitate flight: in vain did Buonaparte collect together, for one last effort, a few battalions of the young and old guard, who had not yet given way, and conducted them once more against the enemy, who had already issued *en masse* from their positions; all was ineffectual; intimidated by what was passing around them, and overwhelmed by numbers, this feeble reserve was speedily overthrown.

At this period the whole army, as if moved by one impulse, abandoned their positions, and retired like a torrent, the gun-

ners quitted their pieces, the soldiers of the train cut away the
traces of the horses; the infantry, cavalry, all kinds of troops
mixed and confounded together, no longer presented the appearance of any thing but an unformed mass, which nothing
could stop, and which was flying in disorder along the high
road and across the fields: a crowd of carriages on the sides of
the road, followed the movement with precipitation, jostling
altogether, and blocking up the road to such a degree, that
there was no longer any passing.

Nevertheless, no cry of *Save who can!* was to be heard, and
this general rout was the consequence of a spontaneous movement, the causes of which are unknown, or which it would
be very difficult to assign, if it were not natural to attribute
them to the account which the soldier knew how to render
to himself, of the perilous position in which we were placed.

The French soldier is never like almost all those of other
nations, entirely passive; he observes, he reasons, and, in
no case, does he yield a blind obedience to his chiefs, so
as to neglect submitting their operations to his own judgment; no point of direction had been given, and there was
no word of command to be heard; the general and other
chiefs, lost in the crowd, and hurried on by it, were separated from their corps; there did not exist a single battalion in the rear of which they could rally; and, since nothing had been provided to insure a reasonable retreat, how
could they struggle against so complete a rout, such a one
as was never heard of, hitherto in the French army, already
assailed by so many disasters.

The guard, that immoveable phalanx, which, in the greatest disasters, had always been the rallying point of the army,
and had served it as a rampart, the guard, in fine, the terror
of the enemy, had been appalled, and was flying, dispersed
among the multitude. Every one now prepared to save himself as he could, they pushed, they crowded; groups, more or

less numerous, formed, and passively followed those by which they were preceded.

Some not daring to deviate from the high road, attempted to force themselves a passage through the carriages, with which it was covered: others directed their course to the right or left, as fancy guided; fear exaggerates every danger, and night, which was now gaining upon them, without being very dark, contributed greatly to increase the disorder.

The enemy, perceiving the confused flight of the army, instantly detached a large body of cavalry in pursuit. While some squadrons, proceeding along the road, fell suddenly on the medical stations, which had not time to be prepared for this assault, other formidable columns advanced on our flanks.

The carriages of the Buonaparte family, seized near the farm-house in which Napoleon had lodged, became almost the first booty of the Prussians, together with a quantity of other baggage. All the cannon which had been formed into batteries, remaining on the ground where they had been used, as well as the caissons which belonged to them, fell at the same time into the enemy's hands. In less than half an hour all the *materiel* of the army had vanished.

The English and Prussians having completely effected their junction, the two commanders, Wellington and Blucher, met at the farm of La Belle Alliance, and concerted the means of following up their good fortune. The English had suffered materially in the conflict. Their cavalry, in particular, being exhausted with fatigue, would have found it difficult to have followed up the French with sufficient vivacity to prevent their rallying; but the Prussian cavalry being fresh, hastened its advance, and pressed closely upon us, without allowing us a moment's relaxation.

The mass of fugitives rapidly passed over the space of two leagues, which divides Gemappe from the field of action, and arrived at that small town, most of them hoping that they should be able to halt there for the night. With the intent of opposing the enemy's progress, they hastened to accumulate carriages in the road, and to barricade the entrance of the principal street.

Some pieces of artillery were formed into a battery, bivouacs were established in the town and its vicinity, and the soldiers dispersed themselves among the houses in search of food and lodging. But scarcely were these dispositions formed, when the enemy appeared. A few cannon-shot, fired at the cavalry as it came in view, spread a general consternation. The camp instantly broke up, each individual took to flight, and the tumultuous retreat was resumed with increased confusion and embarrassment.

During these movements, the fate of Buonaparte was unknown. Some asserted that he had fallen in the combat. When this intelligence was stated to a general officer, he replied in the words of Megret, after Charles the Twelfth was killed at Frederickstadt, *'Thus ends the tragedy!'* It was stated by others, that, after charging several times at the head of his guards, he was dismounted and taken prisoner. The same uncertainty prevailed as to the fate of Marshal Ney, of the major-general, and of most of the principal generals.

The former, who had under his particular command the first and second corps, had personally directed the different attacks at the centre; and had been constantly in the heat of the battle.

It seems that, to the very instant when it became certain that it was not Grouchy's corps which was advancing to the right, he had looked forward with hope for the event; but, on perceiving that Napoleon maintained against all evidence that Grouchy was marching into line, and that he caused this false intelligence to be ostentatiously circulated throughout the ranks, he imputed to him the design of imposing on his troops, and of inspiring them with a confidence prejudicial to their safety.

From that time his opinion changed, and he no longer acted with the same coolness and self- possession: it must be avowed, however, that no reproach was made against him by the army on his change of conduct, and his bravery was never suspected; he merely partook the general anxiety and discouragement. It was, indeed, obvious, that, from the opening of the campaign, he appeared profoundly dissatisfied, but dissimulated his feelings in presence of the public.

Between him and Buonaparte, there existed a certain misunderstanding, and a kind of reciprocal distrust very difficult to fathom, but not the less obvious. There is every reason to believe, too, that he entertained a jealousy of Marshal Grouchy. Such dissensions between the principal chiefs, must necessarily have confined the course of their operations, and disturbed the unity of their plans.

A great number of persons stated that they had seen Buonaparte in the midst of the crowd, and perfectly distinguished him by his grey cloak and piebald horse.

This story was the true one. When the last battalions of the guard were overthrown, Buonaparte was hurried away with then, surrounded on all sides by the enemy, into a cider-orchard, near the farm of Caillou. There he was met by two cavaliers of the guard, who conducted him through the Prussian parties that were scouring the country, but who, fortunately for him, were all employed in stopping and plundering the equipages. In many places he was known and recognized, and often heard the whisper, 'The Emperor!—the Emperor!'— words of alarm, which caused his instant removal from the spot where-ever heard.

After a flight, harassed by the enemy through the whole night, the sad relics of our army arrived about day-break, part of them at Charleroi, and the rest at Marchienne au Pont, where they hastened to re-pass the Sambre. The remaining equipages, impeded by their gradual accumulation on the two roads which lead to the bridges of Charleroi and Marchienne, were overtaken by the Prussians, abandoned by their train and drivers, and thus the last cannon and military-carriage fell into the power of the enemy, who took, at the same time, a considerable number of prisoners.

The Sambre once crossed by the fraction of our army, we expected to be able to halt, and bivouacs were established in the orchards and meadows on the right bank of the river; but an alarm was given, that the Prussians were at hand. Without waiting orders, without attempting to destroy the bridges, without making a single recognizance, the flight recommenced with all its disorder: the whole started at once, and each individual directed his steps he knew not whither.

At a short distance from Charleroi, there are two roads, one leading to Avesnes, the other to Philippeville. Having no instructions as to the route they were to pursue, and not seeing any of their chiefs, the army here divided itself into two parties, the most considerable of which took the road by which they had come, and which led to Avesnes; the other party directed their march towards Philippeville.

A considerable number, cut off from the rest, with no other design than that of escaping the enemy's cavalry, threw themselves into the large woods in the neighbourhood. In this manner did the army become more and more dispersed, and almost entirely disappeared.

It was this last road which Buonaparte had chosen for his retreat. Once more did he desert his army, without making a single effort to rally it, in the midst of dangers which he seemed to delight in, aggravating still more by delivering them up to anarchy, and a total dissolution.

Wandering at random, and issuing in crowds from the woods, thousands of straggling soldiers, spread themselves over the fields, and carried with them alarm and consternation. The unfortunate inhabitants were confounded to learn, almost at the same moment, the success and irreparable defeat of the French army, and to find themselves the prey of an enemy, whom a victory, torn from their grasp, had rendered truly ferocious, at a moment, too, when they were rejoicing to see the theatre of war removing to a distance from them.

The strong places every where shut their gates, and repelled by force the fugitives who presented themselves for admission, obliging them to fall back into the neighbouring communes, where they committed every kind of excess.

It was in his quality of fugitive, that Buonaparte, more confused and less confident than all the rest, came to request admission to Philippeville; he stood in need of the protection of the ramparts of that place to conceal him from the active pursuit of the Prussians, who had tracked him with great caution, and who had already despatched towards this point numerous parties, into whose hands he expected to fall.

On his arrival at the gates, he was obliged to submit to the humiliation of being interrogated by a guard, before whom he laid aside his quality, and who did not allow him admission till he was at length recognised by the governor, who was called upon to identify him. As soon as he had entered with his little suite, the barriers were closed.

A short time afterwards, orders were issued to disperse the collection of soldiers which every moment increased around the city. It being rumoured among them that their *illustrious* emperor was at length found, and that he was in the place, they considered it their duty to encamp around him, flattering themselves likewise, that, through his protecting care, the fortress would at length be opened to them.

Buonaparte, however, was perfectly aware that such a collection of troops might attract the enemy towards this point, and cause his asylum to be discovered; he therefore sent orders to them to continue their route. But having, as an able general, profoundly analyzed the means of acting on the *moral* of his troops after a defeat, in order to insure speedy obedience to his command, he adopted a stratagem, the result of which was certain. A few emissaries, issuing from the town, ran towards the camp in great confusion, crying out, 'Save yourselves, here come the Cossacks; make haste, here come the Cossacks!' It may easily be imagined that more was not requisite, and that the troops instantly disappeared.

This mob of expelled wretches were the persons, who, in despairing accents, and overwhelmed with anguish, circulated the lamentable news, that their emperor was blockaded in Philippeville. This was considered as a positive fact, nor had any person along the roads to Mezieres and Laon the sagacity to conclude that it was nothing more than a well-concerted plan invented by Napoleon to cover the march on which his security depended.

Fortunately, however, the public mind was not long oppressed by the inauspicious rumour of an effect so fatal. Buonaparte left Philippeville after resting some hours there, and proceeded to Mezieres. At the approach of night, he passed by the walls of Rocroi, where it was believed that he would remain. Great numbers of the inhabitants ascended the ramparts, and he had the pain to hear himself hailed with shouts of *Vive l'Empereur!* as long as he continued in sight: he therefore deemed it prudent to take advantage of the night in making the best of his way, and set out as soon as possible. A few only of the officers who attended him, together with the small number of those of his suite who bad survived the disaster, entered the town; two or three horses were all that remained, the carriages of every description having fallen into the hands of the enemy.

The large body of the army, which had directed its course towards Avesnes and Laon, felt the strongest uneasiness for the fate of their emperor; and in this direction, more particularly, they were entirely ignorant of what had befallen him. Con-

vinced, as he was not amongst them, that he must have sunk
on the field of honour, where he had led so many brave men
to death, they mourned over the frightful destiny reserved
for a person so highly valued by them. But on hearing of his
arrival at Paris, in full health and vigour,—eternal disgrace!—
how is the indignation to be described, which could not fail
to impress their minds?

Since the battle of Ligny, all communication with the right
of the army had been cut off; we were perfectly ignorant of
what bad become of them, and the most unpleasant rumours
were circulated respecting them. Where, then, was this fine
army, recruited from the wrecks of many brilliant armies that
Buonaparte had already sacrificed?

It would have seemed that, enraged at seeing a few thousand brave fellows who had escaped his fury, he had issued
from his retreat, only to devour the rest. But the faults that he
committed ought rather to be attributed to his want of skill,
accompanied by an extraordinary rashness, and to his incor-
rigible manner of advancing with a blind confidence, without
any plan, and without calculating on any contingency.

It was evidently from a knowledge of this system of warfare, that the hostile generals laid the snare for him, into which
he plunged himself with such a lamentable security; for whatever foreign journals may say on this subject, with a view, no
doubt, to raise the glory of their generals, and the courage of
their troops, it is evident that the position of Mont St. Jean
had been reconnoitred, designed, and prepared, as the spot
where it was proposed to arrest the progress of Napoleon, and
give him battle.

A man must be like Buonaparte himself, not to perceive
this. The retreat of the English evidently calculated upon so
strong a position: the obstinacy with which they maintained
themselves in it, the facility of masking in an immense forest, troops, and artillery; and, more than all, the batteries they

had thrown up, and which were very apparent, would have inspired any other general with a distrust well-founded, or would at least have made him fear, that this arrangement, instead of being a position arising from circumstances, had been the effect of deliberate choice.

What ought still to confirm this suspicion was, the construction of an observatory of wood, which had been erected on a hillock situate in front of the forest, from which, with a good glass, whatever was passing upon the plain, as far as the Sambre, could be discovered, and which, evidently designed for the purpose of exploring our movements, could not have been erected in the space of twenty-four hours.

With all these hypotheses, did not prudence require the examination of the ground, and of the enemy's positions? would the most inexperienced general have ventured an attack before having insured a communication with his right wing, or, at least, being apprised of the result of its operations? besides, supposing even that the English should be forced, a thing which could not be done without considerable loss, what great advantage could reasonably be expected, since they had in their rear a forest, occupying an extent of fifteen leagues in length, and five in breadth? Ought not the road running through it to be considered as a very narrow defile, where ten thousand men, and a few pieces of artillery, could easily keep the greatest forces in check? Was it then indispensable to attack in front a position naturally very strong? or was there an utter impossibility in turning it?

Such considerations would naturally have presented themselves to the mind of a man the least skilful in the art of war; but Buonaparte was resolved to see nothing upon Mont St. Jean but a numerous rear-guard, already intimidated, who put a good face upon it merely to give time to the different carriages to defile through the forest. He firmly believed, that he was not about to fight a battle, but to follow up his pursuit.

He would neither believe his own eyes, nor listen to the advice of some of the generals, who recommended him to allow the English to effect quietly their evacuation of the forest, or, at least, to wait till the next day for the attack upon them, if they should not have effected it.

Scarcely had his troops come in sight, harassed as they were with the continual rains, than, without allowing a moment of repose, he made them rush on the enemy. Persuaded that nothing could resist them, he made them attack in front an impregnable position, and, disdaining to have recourse to a few manoeuvres, in order to render the approach less dangerous, exposed them with cruel indifference to the destructive fire of numerous batteries.

In a short time he became angry at the resistance opposed to him; and resolving, in his delirium, to force the enemy's line, he pushed on the whole of his cavalry, and obliged them to charge at all hazards. In less than an hour it disappeared, having been overwhelmed by the English cavalry, or mowed down by their artillery. Thus had he deprived himself of the means of following up the pursuit, had he even proved victorious.

Instead of gaining experience from the enormous loss he sustained, respecting the strength and designs of the enemy, and taking means to prevent the total ruin of his army, he descended furiously from the station where he had been directing the operations, placed himself at the head of his guards, and persisted in demanding of them things impossible, until, at length, overthrown and lost in the mass which overwhelmed them, they seemed to vanish, and escaped from his hands in the midst of the carnage.

From that moment all was lost, and the destruction of the army was so much the more inevitable, as its right was turned, and no provision was made for its retreat. Who would believe that Buonaparte was the only man who did not perceive the dangers that menaced him? He still determined on pushing forward; and actually collected all his remaining force to repeat his attempts upon the centre. Inconceivable folly! He cherished the hope of overturnings with a few battalions those forces which had withstood his whole army!

And this is the man who is esteemed *the greatest general of the age!* Undoubtedly he is so, if, to gain battles, it is only necessary to shed the blood of thousands, by making them rush against each other without calculation. Yet it cannot be doubted that Buonaparte has shown at Mont St. Jean the extent of his capacity; victory was there so much needed by him, that he certainly brought his full powers into action.

'Thus we find ourselves reduced to the alternative, either of allowing that he owes all his victories to chance, or that his intellects had forsaken him during the battle of the eighteenth of June; for his combinations on that day can only be considered as well-conceived, by imputing to him the decided intention of causing his army to be massacred. Such, at least, is the judgment formed by some generals, whose ability to appreciate them is unquestionable, who, even during the contest, being unable to recover from their astonishment, or to repress their indignation, exclaimed aloud, 'Surely this man is beside himself! What will he do? His head is turned!'

There are some, however, who are of opinion, that, setting aside every thing relative to the dispositions of the ground, the manner in which he directed the attacks, and the movements which he ordered to be executed, bore a near resemblance to what occurred at Marengo; so that, if suddenly, at the moment when the victorious English forsook their positions to fall upon us, a formidable column commanded by a Desaix had sprung from the ground, it is probable that the affair would have turned in our favour.

If, therefore, Marshal Grouchy had appeared at this instant, be would in reality have performed the part of Desaix, and it is beyond a doubt that victory would have been ours. But he was at too great a distance from the scene of action, to have made so important a figure in it. This consideration is a further aggravation of the unaccountable errors of which Buonaparte was guilty at Mont St. Jean, as he was not, by any circumstances, compelled to attempt so abruptly an affair of such consequence; and as, instead of reducing this right wing to an absolute nullity, by neglecting to make good his communications with it, he might, without inconvenience, have waited until its junction had been effected.

A single day, perhaps a few hours, would have been sufficient for the attainment of this essential object, every probability of success would have been in our favour. Nor, in this circumstance, can the occurrences which happened, be attributed to unforeseen misfortune; since it is evident, that, without the possession of any precise information concerning the march of Grouchy's corps, and of the difficulties it encountered, the measures adopted were such as would have been used, had it been ascertained that the whole Prussian army was fully occupied by that corps, or that it was impossible for any thing to prevent their cooperation, or to impede their movements.

The battle of Mont St. Jean was me of the most sanguinary that was ever fought. The French army composed of one hundred and twenty thousand men, after performing prodigies of valour, was almost entirely destroyed; two hundred pieces of cannon, all the caissons and carriages, fell into the hands of the enemy, as well as an immerse number of prisoners. More than twenty thousand dead bodies of Frenchmen covered the field of battle, horribly mutilated by grape and musketry. The English likewise experienced a great loss, though less considerable than that of the French, on account of the advantageous position they occupied. The whole number of killed, however, in the allied armies, was computed at twenty thousand.

Every circumstance induces us to believe, that, in the beginning, the two armies were of the same force; but the English army was in reality much the strongest, because they waited for us within their entrenchments; and they became still more so by the co-operation of the Prussians at the moment when the affair was just about to be decided.

It was not difficult to foresee the consequences of this battle, and nobody doubted, but that, in a very short time, the allies would be in the capital of France. Nothing could, after this, stop or arrest their progress. The French army, though partly rallied near Laon and Rheims, was too much enfeebled to oppose their march; and they did not fail to arrive quickly under the walls of Paris, where they met some resistance, only in consequence of the arrival of the corps forming the right of the French army.

This right wing, which was supposed to be lost, had retreated with great good fortune by the way of Namur, and, after marching eight days in the midst of the allies, and on a parallel with them, had effected, contrary to all probability, its junction with the rest of the army, without experiencing any material loss.

Seventy thousand men were therefore concentrated before Paris, and threatened to defend that capital. But what was so small a force able to effect against the combined forces of all Europe, now rapidly advancing towards this central point? After a resistance of a few days, highly terrifying to the inhabitants, whose safety was greatly endangered by it, the obstinacy of the troops was overcome. They had resolved on holding out to the last extremity, and conceived themselves entitled to demand the greatest sacrifices.

In gradually disposing them to accept a capitulation, and in thus extorting from them their consent to evacuate Paris, France gained in reality a signal victory, the advantages resulting from which are beyond calculation. It is this likewise, which in all probability preserved the capital from destruction.

The battle of Mont St. Jean, by occasioning the occupation of Paris, and the re-establishment of legitimate authority in France, has been the mean of terminating the frightful struggle in which Buonaparte had involved us. Undoubtedly, the speedy destruction of so many thousands of men is a most horrible catastrophe; but if, on the other hand, it be considered as the prompt and unexpected issue of a dreadful war, to the ravages of which all France was about to be given up for an incalculable period of time, there is reason to believe, that it is in reality the least fatal occurrence which could possibly befall us, in the melancholy situation to which we were reduced.

Supposing, however, that France had been unanimous in her efforts, it would have been impossible for her to resist the force of all Europe united against her. She must necessarily have fallen after a defence of greater or less length, more or less destructive, but, at all events, most disastrous to herself; The decisive results of the battle of Mont St. Jean, therefore, have spared her, if not all the evils, at least a great part of the horrors and calamities into which she would have been plunged, had she become the theatre of an active and sanguinary war.

Life Guardsman Shaw

by E. Bruce Low

Life Guardsman Shaw

Life Guardsman Shaw was looked upon by the citizens of London and of his native county of Nottingham as the embodiment of courage, coolness, and bull-dog tenacity. *Old Shaw the Life Guardsman!* says Dickens in Bleak House, *Why he's a model of the whole British army in himself. Ladies and gentlemen, I'd give a fifty-pound note to be such a figure of a man.* Shaw had come to London from Cossall, his native village, a short time before entering the army; and in an age when pugilism was patronised by all classes, his feats in the prize-ring brought him to the notice of princes and peers, and rendered him the hero of the whole sporting fraternity. In 1807 when he had reached the age of eighteen years he was cordially received into the ranks of the Second Life Guards, where pugilism was then much cultivated. He is described as remarkably large-limbed for his age, and of great muscular strength; he possessed a fair education and held a good character, and it was not long before he was promoted to the rank of corporal, which in the Guards, as is well known, corresponds to that of sergeant in line regiments.

Numerous incidents in his career at this period are still remembered in the ranks. At the beginning of the nineteenth century it was usual for the lower orders to cast vulgar abuse upon private soldiers, and on one occasion Shaw was followed and insulted by a number of strongly built roughs. Determined to put an end to the continuance of this practice towards himself and his fellows, Shaw resolved to tackle the

175

crowd, and soon sent three of their number sprawling into the gutter; but on recovering themselves they again set upon the Life Guardsman. In a few minutes he had dealt out such a lesson to them that the whole crowd was put to flight. He had not again to face such an encounter.

After this Colonel Barton took him in hand and introduced him to the Fives Court, which was regarded as the Carlton Club of pugilism in London. At his appearance in this new arena he was described as follows: 'His height, weight, length, and breadth were of so valuable a nature that, united with a heart that knew no fear, they rendered him a truly formidable antagonist.' The Cockney public, as well as the army officers, took him up, and he soon justified their faith by fighting some of the celebrated pugilists of the day, including Molyneaux and Colonel Barclay or Ury.

It was at this time that he was selected by the well-known artist Haydon to sit as his model for some of his famous paintings. In height he was over six feet, with a fair complexion, grey eyes, light hair, and a round visage, and was so magnificently developed as to be universally admired.

His last prize-ring encounter took place on Hounslow Heath on 8th April 1815, when enormous crowds turned out at early morning to visit the scene of the fight. Shaw had boldly challenged all England for the championship. Three other competitors entered the ring in succession. These were Harmer, Skelton, and Painter. The first two fought twenty-eight rounds before Harmer was declared victor; and finally Shaw found his antagonist in Painter. Of the latter it is related that he had distinguished himself in numerous encounters previously, and had beaten men apparently twice his strength, and, like Shaw, had tackled and overthrown a crowd of bullies who had insulted him at Manchester.

In this encounter with Painter, however, Shaw soon gained the upper hand; and it is reported that although Painter delivered some terrific blows, Shaw seemed to be able to do what he liked with him, and ultimately, after half-an hour's fight, completely overcame his opponent. This victory left Shaw virtually champion of England. Less than a month before this, Napoleon Bonaparte had returned to France from Elba, and Wellington had hurried from the Peace Conference at Vienna, with full powers as Commander-in-Chief of the Allied Army to oppose any movement which 'the little Caporal' might make towards the Rhine or the Belgian capital.

Shaw had henceforth to face the sterner work on the battlefield; for, although his admirers offered to buy him out of the army when the order for foreign service was received, he refused.

If Shaw was the hero of London sportsmen before the war, he became the idol of the whole nation after Waterloo.

After a short period spent in cantonments with the 1st Cavalry Brigade, under Lord Edward Somerset, Shaw's regiment received orders to march to Quatre Bras on the morning of the 16th of June, the day when Napoleon was defeating the Prussian army at Ligny, while Ney was endeavouring to gain a similar victory over the hastily formed advance guard of the British army. Wellington had prophesied, after an inspection of the dispositions of the Prussian army, that it 'would receive a most d——d licking,' and this was amply fulfilled, with the result that the victorious British wing of the allied army was compelled to carry out a parallel retreat, so as to protect the Prussian flank and at the same time cover Brussels.

On the 17th Shaw's brigade saw some fighting with the French cavalry in the neighbourhood of Genappe, when the Guards overthrew the lighter French lancers. Thereafter the retreat was completed without molestation, and the brigade took up a position on the high ground through which the main road to Brussels ran. A corresponding parallel high ridge was soon occupied by the French army. The country has been too often described to necessitate other details being given here; but the reader may be reminded that on the extreme right of the British position lay the chateau of Hougoumont, in the centre the farmhouse of La Haye Sainte, and on the extreme left the village of Papellotte. The Horse Guards were drawn up on the slope in the rear of La Haye Sainte, and here some of the fiercest fighting of the day took place.

As is well known, the soldiers spent the night of the 17th and the morning of the 18th in the greatest discomfort, after their long march from Quatre Bras in the sweltering heat of midsummer. A downpour of rain continued throughout the night in tropical torrents, while the lightning played around them. The men were without protection, and lay upon the muddy ground, rising next morning thoroughly stiff and chilled. Shaw's regiment was composed of tall, muscular men, about six feet in height, and the powerful black horses which they rode exceeded sixteen hands high. Every man wore a brass helmet with a blue-and-red crest and a scarlet- and-white plume on the left of it. Unlike the French cavalry, they had discarded the cuirass. Their dress was a double- breasted red coat, with blue trousers, and they wore a sash of scarlet round the waist. Their arms were carbines, pistols, and long swords. The 2nd Life Guards were commanded by the Honourable Lieutenant-Colonel E. P. Lygon, son of Earl Beauchamp.

At eleven o'clock, when the first cannon-shot was fired, Corporal Shaw was engaged with some of his comrades at a distant part of the field foraging for supplies; but he sharply called together his men, and had joined his regiment before the first cavalry charge was made.

The advance of Prince Jerome's corps on Hougoumont took place about one o'clock; and, while the attention of the British army was directed to that quarter, Bonaparte delivered his first grand attack upon the centre and left of the allied position. The French force employed was of overwhelming strength, and succeeded in producing a panic among the Dutch-Belgian troops who were stationed slightly in advance of the cross-road which marked the crown of the ridge behind which the allied army lay. The attacking infantry force was composed of four divisions from D'Erlon's infantry, Roussell's cavalry division, a division of light cavalry, chasseurs, and lancers, and seventy-four guns. The advance of the French infantry compelled the British battalions to deploy into line; and so soon as this was effected, Roussell's cavalry charged among the allied regiments and cut into a number of them, with the result that the moment appeared so critical that Lord Uxbridge, in command of the British cavalry, was compelled to take immediate action. He ordered the Union Brigade on the left to support Picton's troops, who were being threatened by three French divisions, and he himself determined to lead Lord Edward Somerset's brigade of Guards simultaneously upon the fourth of the infantry divisions, which had reached the British line on the west of La Haye Sainte, and, if possible, to overthrow at the same time the cuirassiers and carbineers composing Roussell's cavalry division.

In the British advance the First Life Guards rode on the right, the Second Life Guards on the left, and the Dragoon Guards in the Centre. Corporal Shaw was in the centre of the left squadron of the Second Guards. Opposed to them was a line of cuirassiers. Both forces were riding at full speed, and neither attempted to draw rein or to avoid the combat. It was remarked that in consequence of the British swords being shorter than those of the cuirassiers, the Guardsmen were forced to wedge themselves in between the files of the enemy before they could strike effectively. This they were able to do exactly as in the Heavy Brigade charges at Balaclava, by superiority of weight and strength. Lord Edward Somerset compared the ringing of the British sword upon the French armour to 'the hammering of so many tinkers at work,' and the noise of the charge was soon mingled with the groans and shouts of the combatants. It was not long, however, before the masses of Frenchmen in the scrimmage were borne down and forced across the ridge by the red-coated Guardsmen. All along the flanks and rear the cuirassiers began to gallop wildly from the field, while the main body was pressed down the ascent to the plain beyond La Haye Sainte. The Second Life Guards rode obliquely through the cuirassiers, who had been checked by the unexpected obstacle of a hidden hollow way (the *chimen creux* of Victor Hugo) cut in the ridge where the cross or *verd cocou* road left the main Brussels road. The Frenchmen sought to regain the high ground, but were pursued by the Life Guards, who came upon them at full speed and compelled a number of the French cavalry to return and seek concealment in the hollow way, in the hope of escaping to the main road. The Second Life Guards, however, pursued them so hotly as to be themselves thrown into confusion by the broken nature of the ground.

It was when the combatants reached La Haye Sainte that Corporal Shaw distinguished himself in a desperate hand-to-hand contest on the level ground adjoining the farmhouse.

Siborne, the official historian of the Waterloo campaign, tells us that Shaw alone slew nine of the cuirassiers in this charge, and there are preserved a number of detailed accounts of his prowess, given by eye-witnesses. On one occasion, mentioned by Sir Evelyn Wood, he was seen to ride straight at a cuirassier who had taken up a position at the junction of the two roads. The Frenchman with his long sword thrust strongly at Shaw below the belt, but his thrust was swiftly parried, and the Life Guardsman's sabre crashed through the Frenchman's helmet, splitting his skull to the chin. In the words of the eye-witness, his face 'fell off like a bit of apple.' At one point two of Shaw's comrades, Dakin and Hodgin, saw him attack the standard-bearer of the cuirassiers, and after a short encounter slay him. When, however, he was about to seize the eagle, he was surrounded by an overwhelming number of the enemy, and lost sight of the trophy in the melee.

Captain Gronow, in his well-known Reminiscences, tells how, at a later stage of this first charge, Shaw again distinguished himself by saving the life of an officer of the First Life Guards.

Having overthrown Roussell's cavalry division, the Guardsmen of the different regiments followed in pursuit, and the British corps had become intermingled. Many of them, in their ardour, had reached the summit of the position occupied by the French, when Napoleon ordered several regiments of cuirassiers and Polish lancers to intercept their retreat by taking possession of the low ground lying between the two opposing armies. Captain Kelly of the First Guards had, with a few men of his regiment, reached the Grand Battery collected by Napoleon in support of his attack, when he noticed the swift approach of the fresh cavalry, and, rallying his men, determined to cut his way back to the British lines. At this moment Corporal Shaw hastened to the assistance of Captain Kelly, and the two riders, riding side by side, headed the returning troopers, and, in the words of a spectator, 'cut down their antagonists as if the latter had been poppies.'

In the retreat Shaw was now opposed by a giant cuirassier in armour. In order to successfully defend himself, he selected the vulnerable part of his opponent, and, parrying his lunges, slew him with a thrust in the neck.

When the remains of the regiment reassembled on the ridges, the heavy losses they had sustained became apparent. Shaw found that the two files which in the morning had stood on each side of him had been slain. He was himself wounded, but refused to leave the ranks.

For two hours afterwards the Guards remained in position inactive under a heavy cannonade. In his official dispatch, Marshal Blücher declares that the decisive moment in the battle occurred at half-past four; and Baron Von Muffling, the Prussian Commissioner on Lord Wellington's staff, states emphatically in his History of the campaign that up to that moment the battle had been 'bloody enough, but in no wise dangerous for the British army.' He adds, 'There was absolutely nothing to fear,' and then goes on to state that 'the position was really more favourable than would appear to Wellington', and that 'from that moment the battle was considered as gained'. The Prussian troops which had been promised to Wellington for the morning of the 18th now showed themselves, so that by half-past four (Blücher's 'decisive moment') two brigades of Billow's corps had appeared before Planchenoit; but, although Sir Evelyn Wood points out that it was after five o'clock before the Prussian cavalry approached the British left wing, Wellington never considered it necessary to call up his reserve of eighteen thousand men stationed between Tubige and Hal, eight miles off.

Wellington's understanding with Blücher had been for the assistance of only one corps and from a greater distance. It cannot be admitted that the arrival of this force saved the British army from destruction, and the later events of the day confirm this, for the British had repulsed and driven off the Old Guard and the whole French divisions of the left wing by eight o'clock, while the Prussians were still engaged on their first point of attack at Planchenoit.

It is true that the German Legion, who occupied La Haye Sainte (and to whose bravery the British writers have done honour) lost the position assigned to them, which had to be retaken by a British line regiment. Unfortunately, also, the King's German Legion, being ordered to deploy by the Prince of Orange, had its flag captured by the French Chasseurs of the Guard, and it was not recovered; but that no reflection can rest upon the British troops in this connection is proved by Houssaye, the latest French writer. There is something grim and sardonic in the fact that the Kaiser should tell the soldiers at Hanover that their countrymen saved the British army from destruction, when we remember that it was the cavalry of Hanover (the Duke of Cumberland's Hussars) which turned tail and fled in disorder to Brussels when ordered by Wellington to move forward to support the British line.

After four o'clock Napoleon, noticing the advance of the Prussian troops, charged Ney with the duty of making a second attack upon the allied position, while he himself directed operations upon his right for the defence of Planchenoit against the new assailants. The French cavalry, led by Ney, approached the British position in three great lines, forty-three squadrons in all (four thousand five hundred horsemen), and soon reached the crest of the ridge where the British batteries lay. There, however, they were met by a tremendous fire, which caused tremendous losses; but the cuirassiers rode gallantly forward to the charge, shouting, *'Vive l'Empereur!'* and *'Victoire!'* They were received at thirty paces with a withering fire from the squares, and were broken up into a disorganised mass, which swept round the squares without charging home. Lord Edward Somerset used this opportune moment for making another advance with the Guards brigade, who, after a very slight resistance from the French cavalry, drove them in confusion into the hollow between the armies, whence after a time they renewed the attack, only, however, to be foiled again. In this way the French cavalry became thoroughly exhausted. Supports were sent for, which were seen moving forward with great apparent determination. Again the diminished squadrons of British cavalry fell upon the advancing troops and sent them headlong to the rear.

Undismayed by these successive defeats, Ney sent for further reinforcements, and obtained thirty-seven squadrons of fresh horsemen, drawn from Kellerman's corps and the heavy cavalry of the Imperial Guards, and then advanced at the head of eighty squadrons to a final attack upon the British right. The reader must be referred to the brilliant pages of Siborne's History and Sir Evelyn Wood's Cavahy in the Waterloo Campaign for details of these successive attacks. Victor Hugo says: 'There were a dozen assaults. Ney had four horses killed under him. Half the cuirassiers fell on the plateau. The conflict lasted two hours.' It ended in the total rout of the Frenchmen. The British squares stood fast, though decimated. Ney, perspiring, his eyes aflame, foaming at the mouth, with uniform unbuttoned, and one of his epaulets cut off, saw the broken regiments returning in complete disorganisation to the French lines.

In these encounters Shaw and his comrades had taken a glorious part, and many are the thrilling accounts left to us of the deeds of the troopers in his brigade. We must, however, restrict ourselves to the narrative of Shaw's last charge.

He had distinguished himself throughout the day, and now, when the British cavalry swept forward and rode through the remains of the French squadrons, Shaw still bore a prominent part, till in the last melee on the level ground to the east of La Haye Sainte he found himself cut off from his companions and surrounded by overwhelming numbers of the foe. The contest was a long one, and it was only when his sword had been broken in his hand that Shaw's defence was overcome. Hurling the hilt of his weapon among the enemy, he tore off his helmet and struck out right and left with it; but the swords of the cuirassiers ultimately cut him down, and he was left for dead on the ground. Victor Hugo tells us that as Shaw lay on the ground a French drummer-boy gave him the *coup de grace*.

That night a comrade, wounded like himself, had taken refuge near one of the houses which line the Charleroi road, and there he found Shaw.

After being rendered unconscious by the many wounds which he had received, he had crept in pain from the open ground to the protection of the farm-buildings which we know as La Belle Alliance. He, we are told, 'was almost cut to pieces and scarcely able to move.' On recognising the other as a comrade, Shaw was only able to whisper, 'my dear fellow, I am done for,' and then fell back from sheer exhaustion. When morning broke his companion found him lying dead, with his face resting on his hand, and having the appearance of having passed away while in a state of insensibility. His death was occasioned rather by the loss of blood from a variety of wounds than from the magnitude of any one. So was ended the career of the best swordsman in the British army, after he had given splendid evidence of his heroism and skill, the memory of which still lives in the ranks of his regiment.

The Greys at Waterloo

Sergeant-Major Dickinson

The Greys at Waterloo

Sergeant-Major Dickson of the Scots Greys was the last who survived of those who fought in the regiment at Waterloo. He enlisted at Glasgow in 1807 when barely eighteen, and remained in the service till 1834. At Waterloo he was corporal in Captain Vernon's troop, and his sabre and other regimentals bear evidence that his number was 57 of F troop. He was promoted sergeant after Waterloo for his services, and took the place of Sergeant Charles Ewart, who received a commission in the Fifth Veteran Regiment for the brave deed narrated here. On retiring from the Greys Sergeant Dickson joined the Fife Light Horse. His army papers bear witness that during his service of twenty-seven years in the Greys his character was 'excellent,' and he was awarded a medal for long service and good conduct in addition to his Waterloo medal.

When I was a lad of eighteen, being a good Scotsman, I joined the Greys, the oldest regiment of dragoons in the British army, and our only Scottish cavalry corps.

When news came that Napoleon Bonaparte had landed in France, we were sent across to Belgium post-haste, and there had a long rest, waiting for his next move. I remember how the trumpets roused us at four o'clock on the morning of Friday the 16th June 1815, and how quickly we assembled and fell in!

Three days' biscuits were served out to us; and after long marches for we did fifty miles that one day before we reached Quatre Bras we joined the rest of our brigade under Sir William Ponsonby.

Besides our regiment there were the 1st Royals and the Enniskillens, and we were known as the Union Brigade because, you see, it was made up of one English, one Irish and one Scots regiment.

On the day before the great fight that was Saturday, for the battle was fought on the Sunday morning, the 18th June, we were marched from Quatre Bras along the road towards Brussels. We thought our Iron Duke was taking us there; but no. In a drenching rain we were told to halt and lie down away in a hollow to the right of the main road, among some green barley. Yes, how we trampled down the corn! The wet barley soon soaked us, so we set about making fires beside a cross-road that ran along the hollow in which we were posted. No rations were served that night. As we sat round our fire we heard a loud, rumbling noise about a mile away, and this we knew must be the French artillery and wagons coming up. It went rolling on incessantly all night, rising and falling.

One thing I must tell you: though there were more than seventy thousand Frenchmen over there, we never once saw a camp-fire burning all the night and until six o'clock next morning. Why they weren't allowed to warm themselves, poor fellows! I don't know. Well, about eleven o'clock that night a fearful storm burst over us. The thunder was terrible to hear. It was a battle-royal of the elements, as if the whole clouds were going to fall on us. We said it was a warning to Bonaparte that all nature was angry at him.

Around the fires we soon fell asleep, for we were all worn out with our long march in the sultry heat of the day before.

I was wakened about five o'clock by my comrade MacGee, who sprang up and cried:

"D— your eyes, boys, there's the bugle!"

"Tuts, Jock!" I replied, "it's the horses' chains clanking."

"Clankin'?" said he. "What's that, then?" as a clear blast fell on our ears.

After I had eaten my ration of "stirabout" oatmeal and water I was sent forward on picket to the road two hundred yards in front, to watch the enemy. It was daylight, and the sun was every now and again sending bright flashes of light through the broken clouds. As I stood behind the straggling hedge and low beech trees that skirted the high banks of the sunken road on both sides, I could see the French army drawn up in heavy masses opposite me. They were only a mile from where I stood; but the distance seemed greater, for between us the mist still filled the hollows.

There were great columns of infantry, and squadron after squadron of Cuirassiers, red Dragoons, brown Hussars, and green Lancers with little swallow-tail flags at the end of their lances. The grandest sight was a regiment of Cuirassiers dashing at full gallop over the brow of the hill opposite me, with the sun shining on their steel breastplates. It was a splendid show. Every now and then the sun lit up the whole country. No one who saw it could ever forget it.

Between eight and nine there was a sudden roll of drums along the whole of the enemy's line, and a burst of music from the bands of a hundred battalions came to me on the wind. I seemed to recognise the *Marseillaise*, but the sounds got mixed and lost in a sudden uproar that arose.

Then every regiment began to move. They were taking up position for the battle.

On our side perfect silence reigned; but I saw that with us too preparations were being made. Down below me a regiment of Germans was marching through the growing corn to the support of others who were in possession of a farmhouse that lay between the two armies. This was the farm of La

Haye Sainte, and it was near there that the battle raged fiercest. These brave Germans! They died to a man before the French stormed it, at the point of the bayonet, in the afternoon.

A battery of artillery now came dashing along the road in fine style and passed in front of me. I think they were Hanoverians; they were not British troops, but I don't remember whether they were Dutch or German. They drew up close by, about a hundred yards in front of the road. There were four guns. Then a strong brigade of Dutch and Belgians marched up with swinging, quick step, and turned off at a cross-road between high banks on to the plateau on the most exposed slope of our position. They numbered at least three thousand men, and looked well in their blue coats with orange-and-red facings.

After this I rode up to a party of Highlanders under the command of Captain Ferrier, whom I knew to belong to the Ninety-second or "Gay Gordons," as we called them. All were intently watching the movements going on about them. They, with the Seventy-ninth Cameron Highlanders, the Forty-second (Black Watch), and First Royal Scots formed part of Picton's, "Fighting Division." They began to tell me about the battle at Quatre Bras—two days before, when every regiment in brave old Picton's division had lost more than one-third of its men. The Gordons, they said, had lost half their number and twenty-five out of thirty-six officers.

Little did we think that before the sun set that night not thirty men of our own regiment would answer the roll-call.

After the village clocks had struck eleven the guns on the French centre thundered out, and then musketry firing commenced away to the far right. The French were seen to be attacking a farmhouse there in force. It was called Hougoumont. I noticed, just in front of me, great columns of infantry beginning to advance over the brow of the hill on their side of the valley, marching straight for us. Then began a tremendous cannonade from two hundred and fifty French guns all along the lines. The noise was fearful; but just then a loud report rent the air, followed by a rolling cheer on our side, and our artillery got into action.

We had one hundred and fifty guns in all; but half of these belonged to the Dutch, Germans, or Belgians, who were hired to fight on our side.

The French had about ten thousand men more than we had all that day, till, late in the afternoon, the Prussians arrived with forty thousand men to help us. I was now drawn back and joined our regiment, which was being moved forward to the left under better cover near a wood, as the shot and shell were flying about us and ploughing up the earth around. We had hardly reached our position when a great fusillade commenced just in front of us, and we saw the Highlanders moving up towards the road to the right. Then, suddenly, a great noise of firing and hisses and shouting commenced, and the whole Belgian brigade, of those whom I had seen in the morning, came rushing along and across the road in full flight.

Our men began to shout and groan at them too. They had bolted almost without firing a shot, and left the brigade of Highlanders to meet the whole French attack on the British left centre. It was thought that the Belgians were inclined towards Napoleon's cause, and this must account for their action, as they have shown high courage at other times.

Immediately after this, the General of the Union Brigade, Sir William Ponsonby, came riding up to us on a small bay hack. I remember that his groom with his chestnut charger could not be found. Beside him was his aide-de-camp, De Lacy Evans. He ordered us forward to within fifty yards of the beech-hedge by the roadside. I can see him now in his long cloak and great cocked hat as he rode up to watch the fighting below. From our new position we could descry the three regiments of Highlanders, only a thousand in all, bravely firing down on the advancing masses of Frenchmen. These numbered thousands, and those on our side of the Brussels road were divided into three solid columns. I have read since that there were fifteen thousand of them under Count D'Erlon spread over the clover, barley, and rye fields in front of our centre, and making straight for us.

Then I saw the Brigadier, Sir Denis Pack, turn to the Gordons and shout out with great energy, "Ninety-second, you must advance! All in front of you have given way."

The Highlanders, who had begun the day by solemnly chanting "Scots wha hae" as they prepared their morning meal, instantly, with fixed bayonets, began to press forward through the beech and holly hedge to a line of bushes that grew along the face of the slope in front. They uttered loud shouts as they ran forward and fired a volley at twenty yards into the French.

At this moment our General and his aide-de-camp rode off to the right by the side of the hedge; then suddenly I saw De Lacy Evans wave his hat, and immediately our colonel, Inglis Hamilton, shouted out, "Now then, Scots Greys, charge!" and, waving his sword in the air, he rode straight at the hedges in front, which he took in grand style.

At once a great cheer rose from our ranks, and we too waved our swords and followed him. I dug my spur into my brave old Rattler, and we were off like the wind. Just then I saw Major Hankin fall wounded.

I felt a strange thrill run through me, and I am sure my noble beast felt the same, for, after rearing for a moment, she sprang forward, uttering loud neighings and snortings, and leapt over the holly hedge at a terrific speed. It was a grand sight to see the long line of giant grey horses dashing along with flowing manes and heads down, tearing up the turf about them as they went. The men in their red coats and tall bearskins were cheering loudly, and the trumpeters were sounding the "Charge."

Beyond the first hedge the road was sunk between high, sloping banks, and it was a very difficult feat to descend without falling; but there were very few accidents, to our surprise.

All of us were greatly excited, and began crying, "Hurrah, Ninety-Second! Scotland for ever!" as we crossed the road. For we heard the Highland pipers playing among the smoke and firing below, and I plainly saw my old friend Pipe-Major Cameron standing apart on a hillock coolly playing *Johnny Cope, are ye waukin' yet?* in all the din.

Our colonel went on before us, past our guns and down the slope, and we followed; we saw the Royals and Enniskillens clearing the road and hedges at full gallop away to the right.

Before me rode young Armour, our rough-rider from Mauchline (a near relative of Jean Armour, Robbie Burns's wife), and Sergeant Ewart on the right, at the end of the line beside our cornet, Kinchant. I rode in the second rank. As we tightened our grip to descend the hillside among the corn, we could make out the feather bonnets of the Highlanders, and heard the officers crying out to them to wheel back by sections. A moment more and we were among them. Poor fellows! Some of them had not time to get clear of us, and were knocked down. I remember one lad crying out, "Eh! But I didna think ye wad ha'e hurt me sae."

They were all Gordons, and as we passed through them they shouted, "Go at them, the Greys! Scotland for ever!" My blood thrilled at this, and I clutched my sabre tighter.

Many of the Highlanders grasped our stirrups, and in the fiercest excitement dashed with us into the fight. The French were uttering loud, discordant yells. Just then I saw the first Frenchman. A young officer of Fusiliers made a slash at me with his sword, but I parried it and broke his arm; the next second we were in the thick of them. We could not see five yards ahead for the smoke. I stuck close by Armour; Ewart was now in front.

The French were fighting like tigers. Some of the wounded were firing at us as we passed; and poor Kinchant, who had spared one of these rascals, was himself shot by the officer he had spared. As we were sweeping down a steep slope on the top of them, they had to give way. Then those in front began to cry out for "quarter," throwing down their muskets and taking off their belts. The Gordons at this rushed in and drove the French to the rear. I was now in the front rank, for many of ours had fallen. It was here that Lieutenant Trotter was killed by a French officer after the first rush on the French.

We now came to an open space covered with bushes, and then I saw Ewart, with five or six infantrymen about him, slashing right and left at them. Armour and I dashed up to these half-dozen Frenchmen, who were trying to escape with one of their standards.

I cried to Armour to "Come on!" and we rode at them.

Ewart had finished two of them, and was in the act of striking a third man who held the Eagle; next moment I saw Ewart cut him down, and he fell dead. I was just in time to thwart a bayonet-thrust that was aimed at the gallant sergeant's neck. Armour finished another of them.'

Almost single-handed, Ewart had captured the Imperial Eagle of the 45th "Invincibles," which had led them to victory at Austerlitz and Jena. Well did he merit the commission he received at the hands of the Prince Regent shortly afterwards, and the regiment has worn a French Eagle ever since.

We cried out, "Well done, my boy!" and as others had come up, we spurred on in search of a like success.

Here it was that we came upon two batteries of French guns which had been sent forward to support the infantry. They were now deserted by the gunners and had sunk deep in the mud.

We were saluted with a sharp fire of musketry, and again found ourselves beset by thousands of Frenchmen. We had fallen upon a second column; they were also Fusiliers. Trumpeter Reeves of our troop, who rode by my side, sounded a "Rally," and our men came swarming up from all sides, some Enniskillens and Royals being amongst the number. We at once began a furious onslaught on this obstacle, and soon made an impression; the battalions seemed to open out for us to pass through, and so it happened that in five minutes we had cut our way through as many thousands of Frenchmen.

We had now reached the bottom of the slope. There the ground was slippery with deep mud. Urging each other on, we dashed towards the batteries on the ridge above, which had worked such havoc on our ranks. The ground was very difficult, and especially where we crossed the edge of a ploughed field, so that our horses sank to the knees as we struggled on. My brave Rattler was becoming quite exhausted, but we dashed ever onwards.

At this moment Colonel Hamilton rode up to us crying, "Charge! charge the guns!" and went off like the wind up the hill towards the terrible battery that had made such deadly work among the Highlanders. It was the last we saw of our colonel, poor fellow! His body was found with both arms cut off. His pockets had been rifled. I once heard Major Clarke tell how he saw him wounded among the guns of the great battery, going at full speed, with the bridle-reins between his teeth, after he had lost his hands.

Then we got among the guns, and we had our revenge. Such slaughtering!

We sabred the gunners, lamed the horses, and cut their traces and harness. I can hear the Frenchmen yet crying *"Diable!"* when I struck at them, and the long-drawn hiss through their teeth as my sword went home. Fifteen of their guns could not be fired again that day. The artillery drivers sat on their horses weeping aloud as we went among them; they were mere boys, we thought.

Rattler lost her temper and bit and tore at everything that came in her way. She seemed to have got new strength. I had lost the plume of my bearskin just as we went through the second infantry column; a shot had carried it away. The French infantry were rushing past us in disorder on their way to the rear, Armour shouted to me to dismount, for old Rattler was badly wounded. I did so just in time, for she fell heavily the next second. I caught hold of a French officer's horse and sprang on her back and rode on.

Then we saw a party of horsemen in front of us on the rising ground near a farmhouse. There was "the Little Corporal" himself, as his veterans called Bonaparte. It was not till next night, when our men had captured his guide, the Belgian La Coste, that we learned what the Emperor thought of us. On seeing us clear the second column and commence to attack his eighty guns on the centre, he cried out, "These terrible Greys, how they fight!" for you know that all our horses, dear old Rattler among them, fought that day as angrily as we did. I never saw horses become so ferocious, and woe betide the blue coats that came in their way! But the noble beasts were now exhausted and quite blown, so that I began to think it was time to get clear away to our own lines again.

But you can imagine my astonishment when down below, on the very ground we had crossed, appeared at full gallop a couple of regiments of Cuirassiers on the right, and away to the left a regiment of Lancers. I shall never forget the sight. The Cuirassiers, in their sparkling steel breastplates and helmets, mounted on strong black horses, with great blue rugs across the croups, were galloping towards me, tearing up the earth as they went, the trumpets blowing wild notes in the midst of the discharges of grape and canister shot from the heights.

Around me there was one continuous noise of clashing arms, shouting of men, neighing and moaning of horses.

What were we to do?

Behind us we saw masses of French infantry with tall fur hats coming up at the double, and between us and our lines these cavalry. There being no officers about, we saw nothing for it but to go straight at them and trust to Providence to get through. There were half-a-dozen of us Greys and about a dozen of the Royals and Enniskillens on the ridge. We all shouted, "Come on, lads; that's the road home!" and, dashing our spurs into our horses' sides, set off straight for the Lancers. But we had no chance.

I saw the lances rise and fall for a moment, and Sam Tar, the leading man of ours, go down amid the flash of steel. I felt a sudden rage at this, for I knew the poor fellow well; he was a corporal in our troop. The crash as we met was terrible; the horses began to rear and bite and neigh loudly, and then some of our men got down among their feet, and I saw them trying to ward off the lances with their hands.

Cornet Sturges of the Royals, he joined our regiment as lieutenant a few weeks after the battle, came up and was next me on the left, and Armour on the right. "Stick together, lads!" we cried, and went at it with a will, slashing about us right and left over our horses' necks. The ground around us was very soft, and our horses could hardly drag their feet out of the clay. Here again I came to the ground, for a Lancer finished my new mount, and I thought I was done for.

We were returning past the edge of the ploughed field, and then I saw a spectacle I shall never forget. There lay brave old Ponsonby, the General of our Union Brigade, beside his little bay, both dead. His long, fur-lined coat had blown aside, and at his hand I noticed a miniature of a lady and his watch; beyond him, our Brigade-Major, Reignolds of the Greys. They had both been pierced by the Lancers a few moments before we came up. Near them was lying a lieutenant of ours, Carruthers. My heart was filled with sorrow at this, but I dared not remain for a moment.

It was just then I caught sight of a squadron of British Dragoons making straight for us. The Frenchmen at that instant seemed to give way, and in a minute more we were safe! The Dragoons gave us a cheer and rode on after the Lancers. They were the men of our 16th Light Dragoons, of Vandeleur's Brigade, who not only saved us but threw back the Lancers into the hollow.

How I reached our lines I can hardly say, for the next thing I remember is that I was lying with the sole remnants of our brigade in a position far away to the right and rear of our first post. I was told that a third horse that I caught was so wounded that she fell dead as I was mounting her.

Wonderful to relate Rattler had joined the retreating Greys, and was standing in line riderless when I returned. You can imagine my joy at seeing her as she nervously rubbed shoulders with her neighbours.

Major Cheney—who had five horses killed under him—was mustering our men, and with him were Lieutenant Wyndham (afterwards our colonel) and Lieutenant Hamilton, but they were both wounded. There were scarcely half a hundred of the Greys left out of the three hundred who rode off half an hour before.

How I escaped is a miracle, for I was through the thick of it all, and received only two slight wounds, one from a bayonet and the other from a lance, and the white plume of my bearskin was shot away. I did not think much of the wounds at the time, and did not report myself; but my poor Rattler had lost much blood from a lance-wound received in her last encounter.

Every man felt that the honour of our land was at stake, and we remembered that the good name of our great Duke was entrusted to us too; but our main thought was, "What will they say of us at home?"

It was not till afterwards that we soldiers learned what the

Union Brigade had done that day, for a man in the fighting ranks sees little beyond the sweep of his own sword. We had pierced three columns of fifteen thousand men, had captured two Imperial Eagles, and had stormed and rendered useless for a time more than forty of the enemy's cannon. Besides, we had taken nearly three thousand prisoners, and, when utterly exhausted, had fought our way home through several regiments of fresh cavalry.

Last Moments at Waterloo
from the journal of Napoleon's
Aide-de-Camp

Last Moments at Waterloo

From two o'clock until a quarter before seven, Buonaparte commanded all the operations and movements from a position where he remained without any danger whatever to his own person; he was a distance of at least a cannon shot and a half from the enemy; nothing in short, could reach him. When he was at length convinced that the *corps d'armee* which he had so long and so obstinately taken for that of Marshal Grouchy, was in reality a Prussian corps, he seemed to think that affairs were desperate, and that he had no other resource than to make a great effort with the reserve of his Guard composed of fifteen thousand men. This he accordingly prepared to do and he assumed an appearance of resolution which re-animated a little those who surrounded him.

He advanced saying, 'Let every one follow me *(Tout le monde en arriere)*' which clearly signified that he wished to be in front. In fact he made this movement at first and headed, for about ten minutes, the formidable column which remained to him as his forlorn hope; but when he arrived within two hundred *toises* (1,200 ft.) from three solid squares of Allied troops which occupied a ridge, with a formidable artillery 'and which ridge it was necessary to carry' he suddenly stopped under the broken ground of a sand-pit or ravine and a little on one side out of the direction of the cannon balls.

This fine and terrible column which he had for some-time headed, found him here as it passed and defiled before him in order to advance, taking a *demi-tour* to the bottom of the hillock and directly in front of the enemy's squares. These Buonaparte himself could not see from the lateral point which he occupied, although it is very true that he was close enough to the enemy's batteries. As the corps passed him, he smiled, and addressed to them expressions of confidence and encouragement.

The march of these old warriors was very firm and there was something solemn in it. Their appearance was very fierce. A kind of savage silence reigned among them: There was in their looks a mixture of surprise and discontent occasioned by their unexpected meeting with Buonaparte who as they thought, was at their head. In proportion as they ranged up the eminence and darted forward on the squares which occupied its summit the artillery vomited death upon them, and killed them in batches.

This part of the scene came directly under Buonaparte's eye, without his being able to see what passed on the height itself as he still kept himself, as it were, enveloped in the corner of the ravine. It was then precisely a quarter of an hour from seven o'clock and it was at this very moment that the decisive crisis of the battle commenced.

Buonaparte had then six persons close to him: these were, his brother Jerome, Generals Bertrand, Drouot, Bernard, Colbert, and Labedoyere. At every step which he took, or seemed to take to put his own person in front Generals Bertrand and Drouot threw themselves before his horse's head, and exclaimed in a pathetic accent: 'Ah! Sire, what are you going to do? Consider that the safety of France and of the army depends entirely upon you; all is lost if any accident happen to you.'

Buonaparte yielded to their entreaties with a real or apparent effort by which he seemed to gain control over himself. But one thing appeared very singular, namely that the two men who knew so well how to moderate his ardour and to restrain him, were the only persons whom he never sent out to reconnoitre the state of the battle, though he sent the others twenty times into the midst of the fire, to carry orders, or bring him information. One of them having told him that the Duke of Wellington had been for a long time in front and at the head of one of his squares, he made a sort of grimace which showed that this part of the narrative vexed him much.

Jerome having thought proper to take aside and whisper with one of his brother Aide-de-camps, to whom he spoke his mind very freely, Buonaparte sent Jerome several times into the middle of the fire, as if to get rid of such an importunate critic.

Jerome, in fact, took it greatly to heart that his brother did not profit by this occasion to die in a glorious manner, and I distinctly heard him say to General Bertrand 'Can it be possible that he will not seek death here? Never will he find a more glorious grave!'

At nightfall Buonaparte disappeared from us under pretext of going himself to ascertain the state of things and to put himself at the head of the Guards to animate them. Before I conclude, there is a peculiarity which deserves to be noticed namely that, before effecting his personal retreat, in order to get rid of impertinent witnesses he directed those around him to carry different orders all at the same time, and to bring information the result of which could not concern him in the least.

Journal of Napoleon's Equerry
the acount of Jardin Aine

Journal of Napoleon's Equerry

12th June: Napoleon left the Elyssee at four o'clock on the morning to join the army, passing by Laon, Avesnes, Beaumont, Charleroi and Fleurus, where the first battle between the French and Prussians was fought. Having reached Laon at six o'clock in the evening he mounted his horse and made a tour of the town and the defences: at eight o'clock he returned to the house of the Prefecture where he lodged.

13th June: At four o'clock on the morning Napoleon again set out for Avesnes, where were his general headquarters. He remained there on the all day.

14th June: Napoleon proceeded on horseback at 10 a.m. to Beaumont where he slept: he rose very early and walked upon the balcony, taking note continually of the weather and conversing with his brother Jerome.

15th June: Napoleon climbed the hill Charleroi, after having driven back the enemy who only surrendered it towards three o'clock in the afternoon. There he made the whole army march past him in column. At seven in the evening he proceeded to the outposts, returning at ten o'clock to sleep at a citizen's house in the Place de Promenade at Charleroi. During the night various officers of the staff kept coming and going to give Napoleon accounts of the movements made by the different army corps. From their investigations they reported to him that General Bourmont had joined the enemy. Napoleon considered it necessary to make fresh plans, being pretty sure that this General from his treachery would give the enemy an exact account of the position of the French army.

16th June: Napoleon left Charleroi at ten a.m. and visited one or two places where he found strong columns of the enemy's army. He continued his observations until a sufficient force had arrived to enable him to commence the battle. Towards three in the afternoon the firing began with much fury and lasted until nine o'clock in the evening when the Prussian were completely defeated. Napoleon spent the evening on the battlefield, until eleven o'clock, when he was assured on all sides that the position had been taken. He passed through the ranks in returning to a village (Ligny) towards Fleurus where he slept. There several of the brave men who had accompanied him from the Isle of Elba, said to him, 'Sire, your majesty has here, far from Elba, the brave men of Elba.'

He replied 'I rely wholly upon you and the courage of the brave army.' On his return in the evening, an infantry Colonel who had just had his arm carried away said to the Emperor, 'Sire, I have one arm less, the other remains at the service of your Majesty.' The Emperor stopped and asked him what regiment he commanded, he replied, 'The first Grenadier regiment of your Guard.'

He was carried to the village with Napoleon's orders that the greatest care must be taken of him.

17th June: Napoleon left the village where he had slept, and visited the battlefield of the evening before as he always did on the day after a battle. He went very quickly up the hill to Genappes where he remained making observations on the movements of his advance guard; the cavalry attached to which several times charged the. British cavalry as it passed out of the town. At this time a violent storm threw into confusion the whole French army which, owing to their many days of rapid marching, lack of provisions, and want of rest was in a most pitiable state. At last the courage of the French overcame the horrible weather. The troops struggled on with unparalleled valour; in the evening Napoleon visited the outposts in spite of the heavy rain and did his utmost to encourage the men. At seven o'clock, he took out his watch and said that the troops had need of rest, that they should take up their positions, and that the next day early, they would be under arms.

At this moment shouts were heard from the British army, Napoleon asked what these could be. Marshal Soult (then Chief of the Staff) replied 'It is certainly Wellington passing through the ranks that is the cause of the shouting.'

At seven o'clock, Napoleon said he wished to bivouac; it was pointed out to him that he was in a ploughed field and in mud up to the knees, he replied to the Marshal 'Any kind of shelter will suit me for the night.'

He retraced his steps and came near the village of Genappes where confusion was at its height owing to the passing of the whole of the Imperial Guard which was hastening to seek shelter from the bad weather. Napoleon went into a kind of Inn out of which the troops, who had installed themselves in it, were turned, and here he fixed his General Headquarters, because he did not wish to go to the town of Genappes, which was only a league distant, saying that during the night he would here receive more readily reports from the army. At the same time everyone had found the best available quarters in which to pass the night. Generals Corbineau, La Bedoyere, Flahaut, Aides-de-camp de-service on Napoleon's staff, spent the night in riding between the various army corps and returning to him to give an exact account of the movements which were taking place.

18th June: Napoleon having left the bivouac, that is to say the village Caillou on horseback, at half-past nine in the morning came to take up his stand half a league in advance upon a hill where he could discern the movements of the British army. There he dismounted, and with his field-glass endeavoured to discover all the movements in the enemy's line. The chief of the staff suggested that they should begin the attack; he replied that they must wait, but the enemy commenced his attack at eleven o'clock and the cannonading began on all sides; at two o'clock nothing was yet decided; the fighting was desperate.

Napoleon rode through the lines and gave orders to make certain that every detail was executed with promptitude; he returned often to the spot where in the morning he had started, there he dismounted and, seating himself in a chair which was brought to him, he placed his head between his hands and rested his elbows on his knees. He remained thus absorbed sometimes for half- an-hour, and then rising up suddenly would peer through his glasses on all sides to see what was happening. At three o'clock an Aide-de-camp from the right wing came to tell him that they were repulsed and that the artillery was insufficient. Napoleon immediately called General Drouet in order to direct him to hasten to reinforce this army corps which was suffering so heavily, but one saw on Napoleon's face a look of disquietude instead of the joy which it had shown on the great day of Fleurus.

The whole morning he showed extreme depression; however, everything was going on as well as could be expected with the French, in spite of the uncertainty of the battle, when at 6 o'clock in the evening an officer of the mounted Chasseurs a Cheval of the Guard came to Napoleon, raised his hand to his shako and said 'Sire, I have the honour to announce to your majesty that the battle is won.'

'Let us go forward,' Napoleon replied, 'We must do better still. Courage *mes braves*: Let us advance! '

Having said this he rode off at a gallop close to the ranks encouraging the soldiers, who did not keep their position long, for a hail of artillery falling on their left ruined all. In addition to this, the strong line of British cavalry made a great onslaught on the squares of the guard and put all to rout.

It was at this moment that the Duke of Wellington sent to summon the Guard to surrender. General Kembraune replied that the Guard knew how to fight, to die, but not to surrender. Our right was crushed by the corps of Billow who with his artillery had not appeared during the day but who now sought to cut off all retreat. Napoleon towards eight o'clock in the evening, seeing that his army was almost beaten, commenced to despair of the success which two hours before he believed to be assured.

He remained on the battlefield until half-past nine when it was absolutely necessary to leave. Assured of a good guide, we passed to the right of Genappes and through the fields; we marched all the night without knowing too well where we were going until morning. Towards four o'clock in the morning we came to Charleroi where Napoleon, owing to the onrush of the army in beating a retreat, had much difficulty in proceeding. At last after he had left the town, he found in a little meadow on the right a small bivouac fire made by some soldiers. He stopped by it to warm himself and said to General Corbineau '*Tre bien Monsieur*, we have done a fine thing.'

General Corbineau saluted him and replied 'Sire, it is the utter ruin of France.'

Napoleon turned round, shrugged his shoulders and remained absorbed for some moments. He was at this time extremely pale and haggard and much changed. He took a small glass of wine and a morsel of bread which one of his equerries had in his pocket, and some moments later mounted, asking if the horse galloped well. He went as far as Philipeville where he arrived at mid-day and took some wine to revive himself. He again set out at two o'clock in a mail carriage towards Paris where he arrived on the 21st at 7 a.m. at the Elyssee.

Certified correct by me,

Jardin Aine

Equerry to the Emperor Napoleon.

The Prussian Perspective

by General Gneisenau

The Prussian Perspective

JUNE 16TH—BATTLE OF LIGNY

The Prussian army was posted on the heights between Brie and Sombref, and beyond the last place, and occupied with a large force the villages of St. Amand and Ligny, situated in its front. Meantime only three corps of the army had jointed; the fourth, which was stationed between Liege and Hannut, had been delayed in its march by several circumstances, and was not yet come up. Nevertheless, Field-marshal Blucher resolved to give battle, Lord Wellington having already put in motion to support him a strong division of his army, as well as his whole reserve stationed in the environs of Brussels, and the fourth corps of the Prussian army being also on the point of arriving.

The battle began at three o'clock in the afternoon. the enemy brought up above one hundred and thirty thousand men. The Prussian army was eighty thousand strong. The village of St. Amand was the first point attacked by the enemy, who carried it, after a vigorous resistance.

He then directed his efforts against Ligny. This is a large village, solidly built, situated on a rivulet of the same name. It was there that a contest began which may be considered as one of the most obstinate recorded in history. Villages have often been taken and retaken: but here the combat continued for five hours in the villages themselves; and the movements forwards or backwards were confined to a very narrow space. On both sides fresh troops continually came up. Each army had behind the part of the village which it occupied great masses of infantry, which maintained the combat, and were continually renewed by reinforcements which they received from their rear, as well as from the heights on the right and left. About two hundred cannon were directed from both sides against the village, which was on fire in several places at once.

From time to time, the combat extended through the line, the enemy having also directed numerous troops against the third corps; however, the main contest was near Ligny. Things seemed to take a favourable turn for the Prussian troops, a part of the village of St. Amand having been retaken by a battalion commanded by the Field-marshal himself; in consequence of which advantage we had regained a height, which had been abandoned after the loss of St. Amand. Nevertheless, the battle continued about Ligny with the same fury.

The issue seemed to depend on the arrival of the English troops, or on that of the fourth corps of the Prussian army; in fact, the arrival of this last division would have afforded the Field-marshal the means of making, immediately, with the right wing, an attack, from which great success might be expected: but news arrived that the English division destined to support us, was violently attacked by a corps of the French army, and that it was with great difficulty it had maintained itself in its position at Quatre Bras.

The fourth corps of the army did not appear, so that we were forced to maintain alone the contest with an army greatly superior in numbers. The evening was already much advanced, and the combat about Ligny continued with unremitting fury, and the same equality of success; we invoked, but in vain, the arrival of those succours which were so necessary; the danger became every hour more urgent; all the divisions were engaged, or had already been so, and there was not any corps at hand able to support them. Suddenly a division of the enemy's infantry, which, by favour of the night, had made a circuit round the village without being observed, at the same time that some regiments of cuirassiers had forced the passage on the other side, took in the rear the main body of our army, which was posted behind the houses.

This surprise, on the part of the enemy, was decisive, especially at the moment when our cavalry, also posted on a height behind the village, was repulsed by the enemy's cavalry in repeated attacks.

Our infantry posted near Ligny, though forced to retreat, did not suffer itself to be discouraged, either by being surprised by the enemy in the darkness, a circumstance which exaggerates in the mind of man the dangers to which he finds himself exposed, or, by the idea of seeing itself surrounded on all sides. Formed in masses, it coolly repulsed all the attacks of the cavalry, and retreated in good order upon the heights, whence it continued its retrograde movement upon Tilly.

In consequence of the sudden irruption of the enemy's cavalry, several of our cannon, in their precipitate retreat, had taken directions which led them to defiles, in which they necessarily fell into disorder; in this manner, fifteen pieces fell into the hands of the enemy. At the distance of a quarter of a league from the field of battle, the army formed again. The enemy did not venture to pursue it.

The village of Brie remained in our possession during the night, as well as Sombref, where General Thelma had fought with the third corps, and whence he, at day-break, slowly began to retreat towards Gambles, where the fourth corps, under General Bulow, had at length arrived during the night. The first and second corps proceeded in the morning behind the defile of Mount St. Guibert. Our loss in killed and wounded was great; the enemy, however, took from us no prisoners, except a part of our wounded. The battle was lost, but not our honour. Our soldiers fought with a bravery which equalled every expectation; their fortitude remained unshaken, because every one retained his confidence in his own strength. On this day Field-marshal Blucher had encountered the greatest dangers. A charge of cavalry, led on by himself, had failed. While that of the enemy was vigorously pursuing, a musket-shot struck the field-marshal's horse; the animal, far from being stopped in his career by this wound, began to gallop more furiously till it dropped down dead. The field-marshal, stunned by the violent fall, lay entangled under the horse.

The enemy's cuirassiers, following up their advantage, advanced: our last horseman had already passed by the field-marshal, an adjutant alone remained with him, and had just alighted, resolved to share his fate. The danger was great, but Heaven watched over us. The enemy, pursuing their charge, passed rapidly by the field-marshal without seeing him: the next moment, a second charge of our cavalry having repulsed them, they again passed by him with the same precipitation, not perceiving him, any more than they had done the first time. Then, but not without difficulty, the field-marshal was disengaged from under the dead horse, and he immediately mounted a dragoon-horse.

On the 17th, in the evening, the Prussian army concentrated itself in the environs of Wavre. Napoleon put himself in motion against Lord Wellington upon the great road leading from Charleroi to Brussels. An English division maintained, on the same day, near Quatre Bras, a very severe contest with the enemy. Lord Wellington had taken a position on the road to Brussels, having his right wing leaning upon Braine-la-Leud, the centre near Mont St. Jean, and the left wing against La Haye Sainte. Lord Wellington wrote to the Field-marshal, that he was resolved to accept the battle in this position, if the Field-marshal would support him with two corps of his army. The Field-marshal promised to come with his whole army: he even proposed, in case Napoleon should not attack, that the allies themselves, with their whole united force, should attack him the next day. This may serve to show how little the battle of the 16th had disorganized the Prussian army, or weakened its moral strength. Thus ended the day of the 17th.

BATTLE OF THE 18TH

At break of day, the Prussian army again began to move. The fourth and second corps marched by St. Lambert, where they were to take a position, covered by the forest, near Frichermont, to take the enemy in the rear when the moment should appear favourable. The first corps was to operate by Ohain, on the right flank of the enemy. The third corps was to follow slowly, in order to afford succour in case of need. The battle began about ten o'clock in the morning. The English army occupied the heights of Mont St. Jean; that of the French was on the heights before Planchenoit; the former was about eighty thousand strong; the enemy had above one hundred and thirty thousand. In a short time, the battle became general along the whole line.

It seems that Napoleon had the design to throw the left wing upon the centre, and thus to effect the separation of the English army from the Prussian, which he believed to be retreating upon Maestricht. For this purpose he had placed the greatest part of his reserve in the centre, against his right wing and upon this point he attacked with fury. The English army fought with a valour which it is impossible to surpass. The repeated charges of the old guard were baffled by the intrepidity of the Scotch regiments; and at every charge the French cavalry were overthrown by the English cavalry. But the superiority of the enemy in numbers was too great;

Napoleon continually brought forward considerable masses, and with whatever firmness the English troops maintained themselves in their position, it was not possible but that such heroic exertions must have a limit.

It was half-past four o'clock. The excessive difficulties of the passage by the defile of St. Lambert had considerably retarded the march of the Prussian columns, so that only two brigades of the fourth corps had arrived at the covered position which was assigned to them. The decisive moment was come; there was not an instant to be lost. The generals did not suffer it to escape. The resolved immediately to begin the attack with the troops which they had at hand. General Bulow, therefore, with two brigades and a corps of cavalry, advanced rapidly upon the rear of the enemy's right wing. The enemy did not lose his presence of mind; he instantly turned his reserve against us, and a murderous conflict began on that side. The combat remained long uncertain, while the battle with the English army still continued with the same violence.

Towards six o'clock in the evening, we received the news that General Thelma, with the third corps, was attached near Wavre by a very considerable corps of the enemy, and that they were already disputing the possession of the town. The Field-marshal, however, did not suffer himself to be disturbed by this news: it was on the spot where he was, and no where else, that the affair was to be decided.

A conflict, continually supported by the same obstinacy, and dept up by fresh troops, could alone ensure the victory, and if it were obtained here, any reverse sustained near Wavre was of little consequence. The columns, therefore, continued their movements. It was half an hour past seven, and the issue of the battle was still uncertain. The whole of the fourth corps, and a part of the second, under General Pirch had successively come up. The French troops fought with desperate fury: however, some uncertainty was perceived in their movements, and it was observed that some pieces of cannon were retreating. At this moment the first columns of the corps of General Ziethen arrived on the points of attack, near the village of Smouhen, on the enemy's right flank, and instantly charged. This moment decided the defeat of the enemy. His right wing was broken in three places; he abandoned his positions. Our troops rushed forward at the *pas de charge*, and attacked him on all sides, while, at the same time, the whole English line advanced.

Circumstances were extremely favourable to the attack formed by the Prussian army; the ground rose in an amphitheatre, so that our artillery could freely open its fire from the summit of a great many heights which rose gradually above each other, and, in the intervals of which the troops descended into the plain, formed into brigades, and in the greatest order; while fresh corps continually unfolded themselves, issuing from the forest on the height behind us. The enemy, however, still preserved means to retreat, till the village of Planchenoit, which he had on his rear, and which was defended by the guard, was, after several sanguinary attacks, carried by storm.

From that time the retreat became a rout, which soon spread through the whole French army, and, in its dreadful confusion, hurrying away every thing that attempted to stop it, soon assumed the appearance of the flight of an army of barbarians. It was half-past nine. The Field-marshal assembled all the superior officers, and gave orders to send the last horse and the last man in pursuit of the enemy.

The van of the army accelerated its march. The French being pursued without intermission, were absolutely disorganized. The causeway presented the appearance of an immense shipwreck; it was covered with an innumerable quantity of cannon, caissons, carriages, baggage, arms, and wrecks of every kind. Those of the enemy who had attempted to repose for a time, and had not expected to be so quickly pursued, were driven from more than nine bivouacs. In some villages they attempted to maintain themselves; but, as soon as they heard the beating of our drums, or the sound of the trumpet, they either fled or threw themselves into the houses, where they were cut down or made prisoners. It was moonlight, which greatly favoured the pursuit; for the whole march was but a continued chase, either in the corn-fields or the houses.

At Gemappe, the enemy had entrenched himself with cannon and overturned-carriages; at our approach, we suddenly heard in the town a great noise and a motion of carriages; at the entrance we were exposed to a brisk fire of musketry; we replied by some cannon-shot, followed by a *hurrah*, and, in an instant after, the town was ours. It was here that, among many other equipages, the carriage of Napoleon was taken; he had just left it to mount on horseback, and, in his hurry, had forgotten his sword and hat. Thus the affairs continued till break of day. About forty thousand men, in the most complete disorder, the remains of a whole army, have saved themselves, retreating through Charleroi, partly without arms, and carrying with them only twenty-seven pieces of their numerous artillery.

The enemy, in his flight, has passed all his fortresses, the only defence of his frontiers, which are now passed by our armies.

At three o'clock, Napoleon had despatched from the field of battle a courier to Paris, with the news that victory was no longer doubtful: a few hours after, he had no longer any army left. We have not yet an exact account of the enemy's loss; it is enough to know that two-thirds of the whole were killed, wounded, or prisoners: among the latter are Generals Monton, Duhesme, and Compans. Up to this time, about three hundred cannon, and above five hundred caissons, are in our hands.

Few victories have been so complete; and there is certainly no example that an army, two days after losing a battle, engaged in such an action, and so gloriously maintained it. Honour be to troops capable of so much firmness and valour! In the middle of the position occupied by the French army, and exactly upon the height, is a farm, called *La Belle Alliance*. The march of all the Prussian columns was directed towards this farm, which was visible from every side. It was there that Napoleon was during the battle; it was thence that he gave his orders, that he flattered himself with the hopes of victory; and it was there that his ruin was decided. There, too, it was, that, by a happy chance, Field-marshal Blucher and Lord Wellington met in the dark, and mutually saluted each other as victors.

In commemoration of the alliance which now subsists between the English and Prussian nations, of the union of the two armies, and their reciprocal confidence, the Field-marshal desired, that this battle should bear the name of *La Belle Alliance*.

By the order of field-marshal Blucher.

General Gneisenau

The Spanish Perspective
Supplement to the Madrid Gazette
July 13, 1815

by Miguel de Alava

The Spanish Perspective

The lieutenant-general of the Royal Armies, Don Miguel de Alava, minister plenipotentiary of his Majesty of Holland, has addressed to his Excellency Don Pedro Cevallos, first secretary of state, the following letter:

Most Excellent Sir,

The short space of time that has intervened between the departure of the last post and the victory of the 18th, has not allowed me to write to your Excellency so diffusely as I could have wished; and although the army is at this moment on the point of marching, and I also am going to set out for the Hague, to deliver my credentials, which I did not received till this morning; nevertheless, I will give your Excellency some details respecting this important event, which, possibly, may bring us to the end of the war much sooner than we had any reason to expect.

I informed your Excellency, under date of the 16th instant, that Buonaparte, marching from Maubeuge and Philippeville, had attacked the Prussian posts on the Sambre, and that, after driving them from Charleroi, he had entered that city on the 15th.

On the 16th, the Duke of Wellington ordered his army to assemble on the point of Quatre Bras, where the roads cross from Namur to Nivelles, and from Brussels to Charleroi; and he himself proceeded to the same point, at seven in the morning.

On his arrival, he found the Hereditary Prince of Orange, with a division of his own army, holding the enemy in check, till the other divisions of the army were collected.

By this time, the British division under General Picton had arrived, with which the duke kept up an unequal contest with more than thirty thousand of the enemy, without losing an inch of ground. The British guards, several regiments of infantry, and the Scotch brigade, covered themselves with glory on this day; and Lord Wellington told me, on the following day, that he never saw his troops behave better during the number of years he had commanded them.

The French cuirassiers suffered very considerable loss; for, confiding in their breast-plates, they approached so near the British squares, that they killed some officers of the forty-second regiment with their swords; but those valiant men, without giving way, kept up so strong a fire, that the whole ground was covered with the cuirassiers and their horses. In the mean time, the troops kept coming up; and the night put an end to the contest in this quarter.

During this time Buonaparte was fighting with the remainder of his forces against Marshal Blucher, with whom he had commenced a sanguinary action at five in the afternoon; from which time, till nine in the evening, he was constantly repulsed by the Prussians, with great loss on both sides. But, at that moment, he made his cavalry charge with so much vigour, that they broke the Prussian line of infantry, and introduced disorder and confusion throughout.

Whether Buonaparte did not perceive this circumstance, or that he had experienced a great loss; or, what is more probable, that Marshal Blucher had re-established the battle, the fact is, that he derived on advantage whatever from this affair, and that he left the Prussians quiet during the whole of the night of the 16th.

Lord Wellington, who, by the morning of the 17th, had

collected the whole of his army in the position of Quatre
Bras, was combining his measures to attack the enemy, when
he received a despatch from Marshal Blucher, communicating
to him the events of the preceding day, together with the incident that had snatched the victory out of his hands; adding,
that the loss he had experienced was of such a nature, that he
was forced to retreat to Wavre, on our left, where the corps of
Bulow would unite with him, and that on the 19th he would
be ready for any affair he might with to undertake.

In consequence of this, Lord Wellington was obliged immediately to retreat; and this he effected with so much skill,
that the enemy did not dare to interrupt him. He took up
a position on Braine le Leud, in front of the great wood of
Soignés, as he had previously determined, and placed in head-
quarters in Waterloo.

I joined the army on that morning, though I had received
no orders to this effect, because I believed that I should thus
best serve his Majesty, and at the same time fulfil your Excellency's directions; and this determination has afforded me
the satisfaction of having been present at the most important
battle that has been fought for many centuries, in its consequences, its duration, and the talents of the chiefs who commanded on both sides, and because the peace of the world,
and the future security of Europe, may be said to have depended on its result.

The position occupied by his lordship was very good; but
towards the centre it had various weak points, which required
good troops to guard them, and much science and skill on the
part of the general-in-chief. These qualifications were, however, sufficiently found in the British troops and their illustrious commander; and it may be asserted, without offence to
any one, that to them belongs the chief part, or all the glory
of this memorable day.

On the right of the position, and a little in advance, was

a country-house, the importance of which Lord Wellington quickly perceived, because the position could not be attacked on that side without carrying it, and it might therefore be considered as its key.

The duke confided this important point to three companies of the English guards, under the command of Lord Saltoun, and laboured during the night of the 17th in fortifying it as well as possible, covering its garden, and a wood which served as its park, with Nassau troops, as sharp-shooters.

At half-past ten, a movement was observed in the enemy's line, and many officers were seen coming from and going to a particular point, where there was a very considerable corps of infantry, which we afterwards understood to be the imperial guard; here was Buonaparte in person, and from this point issued all the orders. In the mean time, the enemy's masses were forming, and every thing announced the approaching combat, which began at half-past eleven, the enemy attacking desperately with one of his corps, and with his usual shouts, the country-house on the right.

The Nassau troops found it necessary to abandon their post: but the enemy met such resistance in the house, that, though they surrounded it on three sides, and attacked it with the utmost bravery, they were compelled to desist from their enterprise, leaving a great number of killed and wounded. Lord Wellington sent fresh English troops, who recovered the wood and garden, and the combat ceased for the present on this side.

The enemy then opened a horrible fire of artillery from more than two hundred pieces, under cover of which Buonaparte made a general attack from the centre to the right, with infantry and cavalry in such numbers, that it required all the skill of his lordship to post his troops, and all the good qualities of the latter to resist the attack.

General Picton, who was with his division on the road from Brussels to Charleroi, advanced with the bayonet to receive them;

but was unfortunately killed at the moment when the enemy, appalled by the attitude of this division, fired, and then fled.

The English life-guards then charged with the greatest bravery, and the forty-ninth and one hundred and fifth French regiments lost their respective eagles in this charge, together with two or three thousand prisoners. A column of cavalry, at whose head were the cuirassiers, advanced to charge the life-guards, and thus save their infantry; but the guards received them with the utmost valour, and the most sanguinary conflict of cavalry that ever was witnessed now took place.

The French cuirassiers were completely beaten, in spite of their cuirasses, by troops who had no defence of the kind; and they lost one of their eagles in this conflict, which was taken by the heavy English cavalry called the Royals.

Intelligence now arrived that the Prussian corps of Bulow had reached St. Lambert, and that Prince Blucher, with another corps under the command of General Ziethen, was advancing with all haste to take part in the combat, leaving the other two in Wavre, which had suffered much in the battle of the 16th, at Fleurus. The arrival of these troops was absolutely necessary, in consequence of the forces of the enemy being now more than triple ours, and our loss having been horrid during an unequal combat, from half-past eleven in the morning till five in the afternoon.

Buonaparte, who did not believe them to be so near, and who reckoned upon destroying Lord Wellington before their arrival, perceived that he had fruitlessly lost more than five hours, and that, in the critical position in which he would soon be placed, there remained no other resource but that of desperately attacking the weak part of the British position, and thus, if possible, beat the duke before his own right was turned and attacked by the Prussians.

Henceforward, therefore, the whole was a repetition of attacks by cavalry and infantry, supported by more than three hundred pieces of artillery, which made horrid ravages in our line, and killed and wounded numerous officers, artillerists, and horses, in the weakest part of the position.

The enemy, aware of this destruction, made a charge with the whole cavalry of his guard, which tool some pieces of cannon that could not be withdrawn; but the duke, who was at this point, charged them with three battalions of English and three of Brunswickers, and compelled them in a moment to abandon the artillery, though we were unable to withdraw them for want of horses; nor did they dare to advance to recover them.

At last, about seven in the evening, Buonaparte made a final effort, and putting himself at the head of his guards, attacked the above point of the English position with such vigour, that he drive back the Brunswickers who occupied part of it; and, for a moment, the victory was undecided, and even more than doubtful. The duke, who felt that the moment was most critical, spoke to the Brunswick troops with that ascendancy which a great general possesses, made them return to the charge, and putting himself at their head, again restored the combat, exposing himself to every kind of personal danger.

Fortunately at this moment he perceived the fire of Marshal Blucher, who was attacking the enemy's right with his usual impetuosity; and the moment of decisive attack being come, the duke put himself at the head of the English footguards, spoke a few words to them, which were answered by a general hurrah, and his Grace himself leading them on with his hat in his hand, they eagerly rushed forward to come to close action with the imperial guard. But the latter began a retreat, which was soon converted into the most complete rout ever witnessed by military men. Entire columns, throwing down their arms and cartouch-boxes, that they might escape the better, fled in the utmost disorder from the field, and abandoned to us nearly one hundred and fifty pieces of cannon. The rout at Vittoria was not comparable to this, and it only resembles it, inasmuch, as on both occasions, the French lost all the train of artillery and stores of the army, as well as all the baggage.

The Duke followed the enemy as far as Gemappe, where he found the illustrious Blucher, and both embraced in the most cordial manner, on the principal road to Charleroi; but, finding himself in the same position with the Prussians, and that his army stood in need of rest after so dreadful a struggle, he left to Blucher the charge of the following up the enemy, who promised that he would not leave them a moment to rest. He is now pursuing them, and yesterday, at noon, he had reached Charleroi, whence he intended to proceed at night, and continue the chase.

This is the substance of what took place on this memorable day; but the consequences of the affair are too evident for me to detain you in stating them.

Buonaparte, now tottering on his usurped throne, without money and without troops to recruit his armies, has received a mortal blow, and. according to the language of the prisoners, no other resource is left him, 'than to cut his own throat.'

It is said that he had never been known to expose his person so much, and that he seemed to seek death, that he might not survive a defeat fraught with such fatal consequences.

I informed your Excellency, under date of the 16th, that this manoeuvre appeared to be extremely daring in the face of such generals as Blucher and the Duke. The event has fully justified my prediction. For this reason, I conceive that his executing it has arisen merely from despair, at the appearance of the innumerable troops who were about to attack him on every side, and in order to strike one of his customary blows before the Russians and Austrians came up.

His military reputation is lost for ever; and, on this occasion, there is no treason on the part of the allies, nor bridges blown up before their time, on which to throw the blame: all the shame will fall upon himself. Numerical superiority, superiority of artillery, all was in his favour; and his having commenced the attack, proves that he had sufficient means to execute it.

In short, this talisman, whose charm had so long operated on the French military, has been completely dashed to pieces. Buonaparte has for ever lost the reputation of being invincible; and, henceforward, this character will belong to an honourable man, who, far from employing this glorious title in disturbing and enslaving Europe, will convert it into an instrument of her felicity, and in procuring for her that peace which she so much requires.

The loss of the British is dreadful, and of the whole military staff, the Duke and myself alone remained untouched in our persons and horses.

The Duke of Brunswick was killed on the 16th, and the Prince of Orange and his cousin, the Prince of Nassau, aide-de-camp to the Duke of Wellington, received two balls. The Prince of Orange distinguished himself extremely, but, unfortunately, although his would is not dangerous, it will deprive the army of his important services for some time, and possibly he may lose the use of his left arm.

Lord Uxbridge, general of cavalry, received a wound at the close of the action, which made the amputation of his right leg necessary: this is an irreparable loss, for it will be difficult to find another chief to lead on the cavalry with the same courage and skill.

The duke was unable to refrain from shedding tears on witnessing the death of so many brave and honourable men, and the loss of so many friends and faithful companions. Nothing but the importance of the triumph can compensate for a loss so dreadful.

This morning he has proceeded to Nivelles, and, to-morrow, he will advance to Mons, whence he will immediately enter France. The weather cannot be better.

I cannot close this despatch without stating to your excellency, for the information of his majesty, that Captain Don Nicholas de Minuissir, of Doyle's regiment, and of whom I before spoke to your excellency, as well as of his destination in the army, conducted himself yesterday with the greatest valour and propriety. He was wounded when the Nassau troops were driven from the garden; yet he rallied them, and led them back to their post. During the action, he had a horse wounded under him, and, by his former conduct, as well as by his behaviour on this day, he merits from his majesty some proof of his satisfaction.

This officer is well known in the war-office, as well as to General Don Josef de Zayas, who has duty appreciated his merits.

God preserve your excellency many years,

(Signed) *Miguel de Alava*

Brussels, 20th June, 1815

P.S. The number of prisoners cannot be stated, for they are bringing in great numbers every moment. There are many generals among the prisoners; among whom are the Count de Lobau, aide-de-camp to Buonaparte, and Cambrone, who accompanied him to Elba.

Wellington's Official Report

Wellington's Official Report

Waterloo June 19th, 1815

My Lord,

Buonaparte, having collected the first, second, third, fourth, and sixth, corps of the French army, and the imperial guards, and nearly all the cavalry, on the Sambre, and between that river and the Meuse, between the 10th and the 14th of the month, advanced, on the 15th, and attached the Prussian posts at Thuin and Lopez on the Sambre, at day-light in the morning.

I did not hear of these events till the evening of the 15th, and I immediately ordered the troops to prepare to march; and afterwards to march to the left, as soon as I had intelligence from other quarters to prove that the enemy's movement upon Charleroi was the real attack.

The enemy drive the Prussian posts from the Sambre on that day; and General Ziethen, who commanded the corps which had been a Charleroi, retired upon Fleurus; and Marshal Prince Blucher concentrated the Prussian army upon Sombref, holding the villages of St. Amand and Ligny in front of his position.

The enemy continued his march along the road from Charleroi towards Brussels, and, on the same evening, the 15th, attacked a brigade of the army of the Netherlands, under the Prince de Weimar, posted at Frasne, and forced it back to the farm-house on the same road, called Les Quatre Bras.

The Prince of Orange immediately reinforced this brigade with another of the same division, under General Perponcher, and, in the morning early, regained part of the ground which had been lost, so as to have the command of the communication leading from Nivelles and Brussels, with Marshal Blucher's position.

In the mean time, I had directed the whole army to march upon Les Quatre Bras, and the fifth division under Lieutenant-general Sir Thomas Picton arrived at about half-past two in the day, followed by the corps of troops under the Duke of Brunswick, and afterwards by the contingent of Nassau.

At this time the enemy commenced an attack upon Prince Blucher with his whole force, excepting the first and second corps; and a corps of cavalry under General Kellermann, with which he attacked our post at Les Quatre Bras.

The Prussian army maintained their position with their usual gallantry and perseverance, against a great disparity of numbers, as the fourth corps of their army, under General Bulow, had not joined, and I was not able to assist them as I wished, as I was attacked myself, and the troops, the cavalry in particular, which had a long distance to march, had not arrived.

We maintained our position also, and completely defeated and repulsed all the enemy's attempts to get possession of it. The enemy repeatedly attacked us with a large body of infantry and cavalry, supported by a numerous and powerful artillery; he made several charges with the cavalry upon our infantry, but all were repulsed in the steadiest manner. In this affair, his Royal Highness the Prince of Orange, the Duke of Brunswick, and Lieutenant-general Sir Thomas Picton, and Major-general Sir James Kempt, and Sir Denis Park, who were engaged from the commencement of the enemy's attack, highly distinguished themselves, as well as Lieutenant-general Charles Baron Alten, Major-general Sir C. Halket, Lieutenant-general Cooke, and Major-generals Maitland and Byng, as they successively arrived. The troops of the fifth division, and those of the Brunswick corps, were long and severely engaged, and conducted themselves with the utmost gallantry. I must particularly mention the twenty-eighth, forth-second, seventy-ninth, and ninety-second regiments, and the battalion of Hanoverians.

Our loss was great, as your lordship will perceive by the enclosed return; and I have particularly to regret his Serene Highness the Duke of Brunswick, who fell, fighting gallantly, at the head of his troops.

Although Marshal Blucher had maintained his position at Sombref, he still found himself much weakened by the severity of the contest in which he had been engaged; and, as the fourth corps had not arrived, he determined to fall back, and concentrate his army upon Wavre; and he marched in the night after the action was over.

This movement of the marshal's rendered necessary a corresponding one on my part; and I retired from the farm of Quatre Bras upon Gemappe, and thence upon Waterloo the next morning, the 17th, at ten o'clock.

The enemy made no effort to pursue Marshal Blucher. On the contrary, a patrol which I sent to Sombref in the morning, found all quiet, and the enemy's videttes fell back as the patrol advanced. Neither did he attempt to molest our march to the rear, although made in the middle of the day, excepting the following, with a large body of cavalry brought from his right, the cavalry under the Earl of Uxbridge.

This gave Lord Uxbridge an opportunity of charging them with the first Life-Guards, upon their debouche from the village of Gemappe, upon which occasion his lordship has declared himself to be well satisfied with that regiment.

The position which I took up, in front of Waterloo, crossed the high roads from Charleroi and Nivelles, and has its right thrown back to a ravine near Merke Braine, which was occupied; and its left extended to a height above the hamlet of Ter-la-Haye, which was likewise occupied. In front of the right centre, and near the Nivelles road, we occupied the house and garden of Hougoumont, which covered the return of that flank; and, in front of the left centre, we occupied the farm of La Haye Sainte. By our left we communicated with Marshal Prince Blucher, at Wavre, through Ohain, and the marshal had promised me that, in case we should be attacked, he would support me with one or more corps, as might be necessary.

The enemy collected his army, with the exception of the third corps, which had been sent to observe Marshal Blucher, on a range of heights in our front, in the course of the night of the 17th, and yesterday morning; and, at about ten o'clock, he commenced a furious attack upon our post at Hougoumont. I had occupied that post with a detachment from General Byng's brigade of Guards, which was in position in its rear; and it was for some time under the command of Lieutenant-colonel Macdonald, and afterwards of Colonel Home; and I am happy to add, that it was maintained throughout the day with the utmost gallantry by these brave troops, notwithstanding the repeated efforts of large bodies of the enemy to obtain possession of it.

This attack upon the right of our centre was accompanied by a very heavy cannonade upon our whole line, which was destined to support the repeated attacks of cavalry and infantry occasionally mixed, but sometimes separate, which were made upon it. In one of these, the enemy carried the farm-house of La Haye Sainte, as the detachment of the light battalion of the legion which occupied it had expended all its ammunition, and the enemy occupied the only communication there was with them.

The enemy repeatedly charged our infantry with his cavalry, and these attacks were uniformly unsuccessful, and they afforded opportunities to our cavalry to charge, in one of which, Lord E. Somerset's brigade, consisting of the Life-

Guards, Royal Horse-Guards, and First Dragoon-Guards, highly distinguished themselves; as did that of Major-general Sir W. Ponsonby, having taken many prisoners and an eagle.

These attacks were repeated till about seven in the evening, when the enemy made a desperate effort, with the cavalry and infantry, supported by the fire of artillery, to force our left centre near the farm of La Haye Sainte, which, after a severe contest, was defeated; and, having observed that the troops retired from the attack in great confusion, and that the march of General Bulow's corps by Frichermont upon Planchenoit and La Belle Alliance, had begun to take effect; and, as I could perceive the fire of his cannon, and as Marshal Prince Blucher had joined in person, with a corps of his army to the left of our line by Ohain, I determined to attack the enemy, and immediately advanced the whole line of infantry, supported by the cavalry and artillery. The attack succeeded in every point; the enemy was forced from his position on the heights, and fled in the utmost confusion, leaving behind him, as far as I could judge, *one hundred and fifty pieces of cannon*, with their ammunition, which fell into our hands.

I continued the pursuit until long after dark, and then discontinued it, only on account of the fatigue of our troops, who had been engaged during twelve hours, and because I found myself on the same road with Marshal Blucher, who assured me of his intention to follow the enemy throughout the night; he has sent me word this morning, that he had taken sixty pieces of cannon belonging to the imperial guard, and several carriages, baggage, &c, belonging to Buonaparte, in Gemappe.

I propose to move, this morning, upon Nivelles, and not to discontinue my operations.

Your lordship will observe, that such a desperate action could not be fought, and such advantages could not be gained, without great loss; and, I am sorry to add, that our's has been immense. In Lieutenant-general Sir Thomas Picton, his majesty has sustained the loss of an officer who has frequently distinguished himself in his service; and he fell, gloriously leading his division to a charge with bayonets, by which one of the most serious attacks made by the enemy of our position was defeated.

The Earl of Uxbridge, after having successfully got through this arduous day, received a wound, by almost the last shot fired, which will, I am afraid, deprive his majesty for some time of his services.

His Royal Highness the Prince of Orange distinguished himself by his gallantry and conduct till he received a wound from a musket-ball through the shoulder, which obliged him to quit the field.

It give me the greatest satisfaction to assure your lordship, that the army never, upon any occasion, conducted itself better. The division of guards, under Lieutenant-general Cooke, who is severely wounded, Major-general Maitland, and Major-general Byng, set an example which was followed by all; and there is no officer, nor description of troops, that did not behave well.

I must, however, particularly mention, for his royal highness's approbation, Lieutenant-general Sir H. Clinton; Major-general Adam; Lieutenant-general Charles Baron Alten, severely wounded; Major-general Sir Colin Halket, severely wounded; Colonel Ompteda; Colonel Mitchele, commanding a brigade of the fourth division; Major-generals Sir James Kempt and Sir Denis Pack; Major-general Lambert; Major-general Lord E. Somerset; Major-general Sir W. Ponsonby; Major-general Sir C. Grant, and Major-general Sir H. Vivian; Major-general Sir O. Vandeleur; Major-general Count Dornberg. I am also particularly indebted to General Lord Hill, for his assistance and conduct upon this, as upon all former occasions.

The artillery and engineer departments were conducted much to my satisfaction by Colonel Sir G. Wood, and Colonel Smyth; and I had every reason to be satisfied with the conduct of the Adjutant- general Major-general Barnes, who was wounded, and of the Quarter-master-general, Colonel Delancy, who was killed by a cannon-shot in the middle of the action. This officer is a serious loss to his majesty's service, and to me at this moment. I was likewise much indebted to the assistance of Lieutenant-colonel Lord Fitzroy Somerset, who was severely wounded, and of the officers composing my personal staff, who have suffered severely in this action. Lieutenant-colonel the honourable Sir Alexander Gordon, who has died of his wounds, was a most promising officer, and is a serious loss to his majesty's service.

General Kruse, of the Nassau service, likewise conducted himself much to my satisfaction, as did General Trip, commanding the heavy brigade of cavalry, and General Vanhope, commanding a brigade of infantry of the king of the Netherlands.

General Pozzo di Borgo, General Baron Vincent, General Muffling, and General Alava, were in the field during the action, and rendered me every assistance in their power. Baron Vincent is wounded, but I hope not severely; and General Pozzo di Borgo received a contusion.

I should not do justice to my feelings, or to Marshal Blucher and the Prussian army, if I did not attribute the successful result of this arduous day to the cordial and timely assistance received from them.

The operation of General Bulow upon the enemy's flank, was a most decisive one, and, even if I had not found myself in a situation to make the attack which produced the final result, it would have forced the enemy to retire, if his attacks should have failed, and would have prevented him from taking advantage of them, if they should unfortunately have succeeded.

I send, with this despatch, two eagles, taken by the troops in this action, which Major Percy will have the honour of laying at the feet of his Royal Highness. I beg leave to recommend him to your lordship's protection.

I have the honour, &c.

Wellington

Waterloo

D. H. Parry

Waterloo

It was the month of June, and the weather was intensely warm. An army under Wellington, some 100,000 strong, including British King's German Legion, Hanoverian, Brunswick, Dutch, Belgian, and Nassau troops, was distributed in cantonments from the Scheldt to the Charleroi *chaussée*.

It was a heterogeneous force, hastily got together, and a large proportion of it by no means to be depended upon.

Of the British regiments, many were formed of weak second and third battalions which had never been under fire, and nearly 800 militiamen fought in the ranks of the 3rd Guards and 42nd Highlanders, those in the Guards actually wearing their Surrey jackets.

Blücher's force, seasoned veterans for the most part, lay in four separate corps on the frontier south of Brussels, and so masterly were Napoleon's that until the lights of his bivouac fires were suddenly seen glowing redly in the darkness beyond Charleroi, no one knew exactly where he was.

Brussels swarmed with fashionable folk, and the families of officers who were with the army.

The Duchess of Richmond gave a ball on the night of the 15th June, the list of invited guests being curious, and not a little melancholy. Among the two hundred odd names we read those of Wellington, Uxbridge, and Hussey Vivian: two Ponsonbys, one of whom was to die three days later; Hay, the handsome lad who had won a sweepstake at Grammont the Tuesday before, and whose young life ebbed out on the Friday at Quatre Bras; Cameron, of Fassifern, who also fell there Dick of the 42nd, killed at Sobraon in '46; and aide-de-camp Cathcart, who lived till Inkerman, where a ball and three bayonet thrusts closed his strange career. These and many others of more or less note danced in the long, low-roofed, barn-like room which His Grace of Richmond had hired for the occasion from his neighbour, Van Asch, the coachbuilder.

About midnight Wellington, having already learned that the outposts had been engaged, went to the ball, where he found the Prince of Orange. Now, the Prince of Orange, who seemed fated to cause the useless sacrifice of valuable life, ought to have been at his post at Binche, and thither the duke promptly sent him, after first inquiring if there were any news.

"No, nothing, but that the French have crossed the Sambre, and had a brush with the Prussians!" Müffling had previously brought the intelligence, which should have arrived much sooner, the duke afterwards saying to Napier: "I cannot tell the world that Blücher picked the fattest man in his army to ride with an express to me, and that he took thirty hours to go thirty miles."

Far from being surprised (as some writers have it), the duke's orders were despatched before he went to that now historic entertainment, and the dancing continued long after he and his officers had left.

At two o'clock, while it was yet dark, strange sounds were heard under the trees—the shuffling of men's feet, the ringing of musket-butts on the ground, short words of command, and the running ripple of the roll-call along the ranks.

People opened their windows and looked out carriages returning from the ball drew up and waited: it was Picton's Division off to the front.

At four o'clock Pack's Highlanders, in kilt and feather bonnet, swung across the Place Royale and passed through the Namur Gate—the rising sun glinting on their accoutrements, their bagpipes waking the sleeping streets. "Come to me and I will give you flesh," was the weird *pibroch* of the Black Watch, and many a Highland laddie heard it that morning for the last time.

Some of the officers marched in silk stockings and dancing-pumps. Lingering too long at the ball, they had not had time—or perhaps, as the night was warm, they had not troubled—to change them; and there were not a few who never found time again.

Out in the early morning along the great highway they went, past lonely farms and clustering villages, through the grey-green gloom of the beech woods of Soigne to Mont St. Jean, where they halted for breakfast, and where about eight the duke passed them with his staff, leaving strict orders to keep the road clear, and at noon the troops were on the march again for Quatre Bras, which was the fiery prelude to the greatest battle fought in modern times.

The heat was so intense that one man of the 95th Rifles went mad, and fell dead in the road; but the others pushed on, and were soon afterwards under fire.

If you take a map of Belgium, placing your finger on Brussels, and pass it down the great road running south, you will find, some twelve miles from the capital, the village of Mont St. Jean; a little beyond which place a cross-road from Wavre intersects the *chaussée*, and at that point move your finger at right angles, right and left, for a mile or so each way, and you have, roughly, the English position on the 18th June.

Continuing again, still southward, you will pass La Belle Alliance and Genappe, and nine miles from the cross-roads before Mont St. Jean is Quatre Bras.

Rolling ridges of waving grain, some woods in all their summer beauty, a gabled farmhouse, and a few cottages where four ways meet—that is one's impression of Quatre Bras, which Ney had orders to take, and drive out Perponcher's Dutch Belgians posted there; but we arrived to their assistance, corps after corps, at intervals, and forming up in line and square, repulsed the Cuirassiers and Lancers who charged through the tall rye.

The crops were so high that the gallant French cavalry had to resort to a curious device in singling out our regiments. A horseman would dash forward, find out the position, plant a lance in the ground, and disappear; then, in a few moments, guided by the fluttering pennon, his comrades would burst upon us—invisible until within a few horse-lengths.

Waterloo has put Quatre Bras into the shade, but few conflicts have been more brilliant.

Our 69th—thanks to Orange, who interfered with its formation just as the 8th Cuirassiers came through the corn—lost its only colour, taken by Trooper Lami, although Volunteer Clarke received twenty-three wounds and lost the use of an arm in its defence.

The 69th's other colour had been captured at Bergen-op-Zoom, and was hung in the Invalides.

By four o'clock the 44th had upwards of 16 officers and 200 men killed and wounded.

A grey-headed French lancer drove his point into Ensign Christie's left eye, down through his face, piercing his tongue and entering the jaw but in that shocking condition he still stuck manfully to the colour-pole, until, finding himself overpowered, he threw the colour down and lay upon it, and some privates of the regiment closing round the Frenchman, lifted him out of his saddle on their bayonet points!

The 92nd Highlanders—the old Gordons of Peninsular fame—were the last of Picton's men to reach the field, and were formed up in line.

"Ninety-second, don't fire till I tell you!" cried Wellington, as a mass of Cuirassiers charged them in his presence; and the word was not given until the dashing horsemen were within twenty yards.

A little later, the duke said again: "Now, 92nd, you must charge these two columns of infantry"; and charge they did, over a ditch, driving the French before them, but their beloved colonel, Cameron, received a death-wound from the upper windows of a house.

His horse turned and bolted with him, back along the road, until he came to his master's groom holding a second mount, when, stopping suddenly, the dying man was pitched on his head on to the stone causeway. But he had been terribly avenged; for the kilted Highlandmen burst into the house with a roar and put every soul inside to the bayonet.

"Where is the rest of the regiment?" asked Picton in the evening. Alas! upwards of half the "gay Gordons" had perished in the fray.

Through the broiling heat of that summer day our infantry stood firm, growing stronger as regiment after regiment arrived, and fresh batteries unlimbered in the trampled corn, until at night Ney fell back, leaving us in possession; our cavalry came up, jaded by their long marches and we bivouacked on the battlefield, cooking our suppers in the cuirasses of the slain.

Meanwhile, Napoleon had beaten Blücher a few miles away at Ligny, but had neglected, in most un-Napoleonic fashion, to follow up his advantage, and the wily old hussar—he was over seventy-three—slipped off in the dark and retreated on Wavre.

When Wellington learned this next morning, he said to Captain Bowles: "Old Blücher has had a—good licking, and has gone back to Wavre. As he has gone back, we must go too. I suppose in England they will say we have been licked. I can't help that." So back we went, along the Brussels road, our cavalry covering the retreat until we reached the stronger position before Mont St. Jean, where we halted and faced about, and glued ourselves on the ridge across the causeway in such a manner that all the magnificent chivalry of France could never move us.

During the retreat from Quatre Bras on the 17th, all went well until the middle of the day. The wounded had been collected; the, columns filed off along the road; one of the regiments even found time to halt and flog a marauder: when, the enemy's cavalry pressing our rearguard too closely, some Horse Artillery guns opened fire, and the discharge seemed to burst the heavy rain clouds.

It poured down in torrents; roads were turned into watercourses. The fields and hollows became swamps; we had a smart brush with some Lancers at Genappe, where our 7th Hussars and 1st Life Guards charged several times; the 10th Hussars had also occasion to dismount some men and line a hedgerow with their carbines; but the main feature of the retreat was a weary tramp in a deluge of rain. The cavalry, had their cloaks, it is true, but the greatcoats of the foot soldiers had been sent back to England. Soaked to the skin, we arrived at the ridge above La Haye Sainte, and prepared to pass the night without covering of any kind. The French advanced almost up to us, and Captain Mercer was giving them a few rounds from his 9-pounders when a man in a shabby old drab overcoat and rusty round hat strolled towards him and began a conversation. Mercer, who thought him one of the numerous amateurs with whom Brussels was swarming, answered curtly enough, and the stranger went away.

That shabby man was General Picton, who fell next day on the very spot where he received this unmerited snubbing. He fought at Quatre Bras in plain clothes, having joined the army hurriedly in advance of his baggage, and there is good reason to believe that he wore the same dress at Waterloo.

Now commenced preparations for a dismal bivouac. The French fell back and did not disturb us again, they too suffering from the drenching rain, which beat with a melancholy hissing on the cornfields, the clover, the potato patches and ploughed land which formed both positions.

Some of our officers found shelter in neighbouring cottages; Lord Uxbridge, afterwards Marquis of Anglesey, crept into a piggery and sipped tea with Waymouth of the 2nd Life Guards; but most of them cowered with their men round wretched fires which here and there were coaxed into burning.

One of Mercer's lieutenants had an umbrella, which had caused much merriment during the march, but he and his captain found it a haven of refuge under the lee of a hedge that night.

The cavalry stood to their horses, cloaked, with one flap over the saddle; some few were lucky enough to get a bundle of straw or pea-sticks to sit down upon, and all looked anxiously for the dawn—fated to prove the last to thousands of them. With morning the rain gradually declined to a drizzle, which finally ceased; fires sprang up, arms were cleaned, and a buzz of voices rose along the line as tall Lifeguardsmen went down behind La Haye Sainte to dig potatoes, where, a few hours later, they were charging knee to knee, and every one made shift to get what he could—with most it was only a hard biscuit—and to dry himself, which was a still more difficult matter.

Wet to the skin, splashed from head to foot in mud and mire, cold, shivering, unshaven (the foundation laid of acute rheumatism, to which a pension of five pence a day, in some cases ten pence, was applied by a grateful country, to its indelible disgrace), such was the condition of those brave hearts who were about to make the name of "Waterloo-man" a household word for all the ages.

The Brussels road runs across a shallow valley, three-quarters of a mile in width, all green and golden with the ripening grain, dipping sharply into it by the white-walled, blue-roofed farmstead of La Haye Sainte, and rising gently out again at the cabaret of La Belle Alliance on its way to the frontier beyond Charleroi.

The valley is bounded by two ridges: on the northern one along the cross road which runs nearly the whole length of the position, our army was posted in the form of a thin crescent; on the southern ridge and the slopes leading down into the valley the French forces were afterwards distributed, also, to some extent, in crescent shape.

These crescents had their tips advanced towards each other, and enclosed in the oval thus formed were two important strongholds—La Haye Sainte, in advance of our left centre and the château of Hougoumont, some distance in front of our right wing; while away to the extreme left, the white buildings of Papelotte partly concealed Ter La Haye farm and the red-tiled hamlet of Smohain, the end of our line in that direction.

The cross-road which I have mentioned as lying along our position, and which was the celebrated "sunken road of Ohain," runs in some place between banks, at others on the level; it is paved down its centre, like most Belgian roads, with irregular stones, terrible to traverse for any distance, and it undulates gently, as the ridge rises and falls, until it joins the Nivelle *chaussée* beyond Hougoumont. Hougoumont, surrounded by a quadrangle of tall trees, lies in a hollow in front of our ridge, perhaps halfway between it and the enemy's line. A Flemish château with a garden laid out in the French style, and a smaller garden full of currant bushes; barns and quaint outbuildings clustering round the château, a brick wall about the height of a tall man, built on lower courses of grey stone, enclosing the garden, and at the east end of it a large open orchard; from the north-west corner, an avenue of ancient poplars winding into the Nivelle road with an abattis of tree trunks there, held by a company of the 51st Light Infantry; between the south wall and the French, a beech wood, through which one could see the corn-clad slopes beyond and that was Hougoumont on the day of the battle.

The beech wood has been cut down, the apple-trees are sparse and scanty now, the château was burned by the French shells, and the garden is a grassy paddock; but the rest remains, loopholed and pockmarked with balls, a monument to the gallantry of two brave nations. The light companies of the Foot Guards occupied it on the 17th, and all night long they, were busy, boring walls, barricading the gateways and erecting platforms from which to pour their fire.

On the high ground behind Hougoumont on our side the 2nd Brigade of British Guards was posted, having Maitland's Guards on its left; beyond Maitland was Alten's Infantry and Kielmansegge's Hanoverians, flanked in their turn by the gallant King's German Legion, in the pay of England, whose left rested on the Brussels *chaussée*, behind La Haye Sainte. On the other side of the *chaussée* was Kempt, then Pack's Highlanders, the Royal Scots, and 44th Regiment, some more Hanoverians, under Best, the 5th Hanoverians of Vincke, Vandeleur's Light Dragoons, and Vivian's Hussar Brigade.

The 2nd Rifles of the German Legion held La Have Sainte, three companies of our 95th occupying a knoll and sandpit on the other side of the road, and Papelotte was garrisoned by Dutch Belgians, who behaved with the greatest gallantry.

Along the front of this, our first fighting line, the artillery was posted at intervals, and sufficient justice has not been done to the brave gunners, the duke always being unfairly severe on that arm of the service. Our heavy cavalry stood, in hollows behind the line, right and left of the great road in front of the farm of Mont St. Jean, already full of the Quatre Bras wounded. Other troops were in reserve out of sight of the enemy, behind our ridge, ready to advance and fill up any gaps, and we had a strong force in and about Braine l'Alleud, two miles to our right, in case the French should try to turn us there.

Crops, as at Quatre Bras, covered the valley and ridges, and the whole plain undulated in every direction. The battlefield to-day is full of surprises. Sudden dips occur where the land seems flat from a little distance; tongues of ground and barley-covered hillocks rise expectedly as you approach them; and it is possible to lose sight of the entire field by a few yards of walking in some directions; so that, flat as Belgium is generally considered, it is not astonishing that the survivors of Waterloo could only speak to events in their own immediate vicinity.

Between nine and ten there was loud cheering, as the Duke of Wellington rode along the line with his Staff. He wore a blue frock coat, white cravat, and buckskin breeches, with tasselled Hessian boots; a short blue cloak with a white lining, and a low cocked hat with the British black cockade, and three smaller ones, for Spain, Portugal, and the Netherlands. He was mounted on his favourite chestnut, Copenhagen, a grandson of Eclipse, and carried a long field-telescope drawn out for use.

At nine o'clock there was a movement on the opposite side of the valley; columns debouched into the fields right and left of the *chausée*, and took up their positions as orderly as if upon parade; glittering files of armoured Cuirassiers trotted through the corn, and formed behind the infantry, lance-pennons fluttered on each flank, and by half-past ten 61,000 French soldiers were drawn up in battle array, their right opposite Papelotte, their centre at La Belle Alliance, their left wing somewhat beyond Hougoumont.

The two greatest living commanders were about to measure swords for the first and only time; and as Napoleon galloped along his line, the music of the French bands was distinctly heard; helmets and weapons were brandished in the air, and a shout of *"Vive l'Empereur!"* rolled across the field.

Blue-coated infantry formed their first ranks, with batteries of brass cannon dotted here and there; behind stood the heavy cavalry with more guns, supported, on their right, by the gay light horse of the Guard, on the left by the heavy cavalry of the Imperial cohort, and in rear of the centre about the farm of Rossomme, stood the invincible infantry of the Guard, the most renowned body of warriors in Europe.

Napoleon was unwell.

At two in the morning he had been reconnoitring, and his horses were ordered for seven; at ten he still sat in an upper room in an attitude of bodily and mental suffering.

A little later he came down the steep ladder, and as his page, Gudin, was helping him into the saddle he lifted the Imperial elbow too suddenly, and Napoleon pitched over on the offside, nearly coming to the ground.

"*Allez*," he hissed, "*à tous les diables!*" and away he started in a great rage.

The page stood watching the *cortée* with tearful eyes, but when it had gone some hundred yards the ranks of the Staff opened, and Napoleon came riding back alone.

With one hand placed tenderly on the lad's shoulder he said, very softly, "My child, when you assist a man of my girth to mount, it is necessary to proceed more carefully." Yet it was of this man that Wellington could say, in after years, "The fellow was no gentleman!"

There was a lull before the storm, and the duke went to have a final look at Hougoumont, where, in addition to the Guards, he had posted in the woods and grounds, some Nassauers Hanoverians, and Luneberg riflemen.

These foreigners were dissatisfied at their position, and as Wellington rode away several bullets came whistling after him! "How can they expect me to win a battle with troops like those?" was his only comment.

About half-past eleven came the First Attack!

One booming cannon echoed dully in the misty Sabbath morning, and a cloud of dark-blue skirmishers ran forward against Hougoumont, firing briskly into the wood.

Puffs of white smoke issued from the trees; here and there a bluecoat turned a somersault and lay still; but the cloud increased, and a loud rattle of musketry was kept up on both sides, which lasted, with short intervals, the whole day.

Our men fell back upon the buildings through open beech-trees, and in twenty minutes the French supporting columns were pouring up the hill towards the château grounds.

Cleeve's German battery opened on them, and his first shot killed seventeen men, the guns checking the advance and sending the column, broken and bleeding, down the ridge again.

Our batteries on the right now began; the French artillery replied; Kellermann's horse batteries joined in, and the infernal concert was in full blast.

The green Lunebergers and the yellow knapsacks of the Hanoverians came helter-skelter back across the orchard, but the Foot Guards went forward at a run and drove the enemy off.

Bull's howitzers sent a shower of 5½-inch shells over the château into the wood, and as often as the death-dealing globes fell crashing through the branches, so often did the enemy retire in confusion, until Jérôme Bonaparte, ex-king of Westphalia, who was in command at Hougoumont, brought up Foy's Division to help the attack.

Bravely led by their officers, the tall shakoes and square white coat-facings of the line regiments, the dark-blue and black gaiters of the light infantry, pressed through the wood until they reached a stiff quickset hedge, separated by a thin strip of apple orchard from the long south wall, over which peeped the head-gear of our Guardsmen, and in the confusion of smoke and skirmish the bright-red brickwork was mistaken for a line of British—you can see to-day where the French balls crumbled that barrier. But soon discovering their error, the brave fellows struggled through the hedge and rushed forward.

A line of loopholes perforated the wall about three feet from the ground, crossed bayonets protruded viciously from the openings, and a hail of bullets poured forth with such ghastly effect that in half-an-hour there were fifteen hundred of God's creatures dead and dying on the green grass in this orchard, and still the others came on.

Some got as far as the loopholes, and seized the bayonets; others struck with their gun butts at the men, who, on platforms behind the wall, fired down over the top, piling up the dead in dreadful heaps—privates and officers, conscripts and veterans.

From time to time our Foot Guards charged over the large orchard at the east end of the enclosed garden, and also at the south-west angle of the farm buildings, where a haystack helped to cover them until the French burned it; and this repulse and attack went on, time and again, until the evening, the enemy gaining no advantage but the beech wood for all their desperate valour.

The rest of our line had remained passive listeners to the firing, except for a little skirmishing here and there, but a hurricane was brewing and about to burst against our left and centre.

La Haye Sainte was a farm, lying like Hougoumont in a hollow; it was on the Brussels road, and was built with barn and stabling round three sides of an oblong yard, the fourth side being a high white wall, with a gate and a piggery alongside the roadway.

Towards the French position stretched a long orchard, a small garden lay behind the house, and a large double door opened from the yard into the fields on the Hougoumont side, half of which door had been burned for bivouac fires the night previous. The 2nd Rifles of the German Legion, dressed like our own in green with slate-coloured pantaloons, held the post, and held it like the heroes of old, three companies in the orchard, two in the building, and one in the garden, Major Baring, who had two horses shot under him, being in command.

The post was not as strong as Hougoumont, all the pioneers having been sent to fortify the latter place, and the "Green Germans" had a very insufficient supply of ammunition; Wellington afterwards admitting that he had neglected to make the most of the position there.

At 1.30 p.m. Marshal Ney had gathered seventy-four guns, mostly 12-pounders, on a ridge very near to La Haye Sainte on the French right of the road, and this was known as the "Great Battery."

Behind the guns the whole of D'Erlon's Corps, together with Bachelu's Division, was massed in columns for the attack—twenty regiments, Bachelu being in reserve. Ney sent to the Emperor to tell him all was ready, and with an appalling cannonade on our left and centre, they commenced the Second Attack.

When the smoke which hung about the guns had drifted slowly away across the slopes we could see four massive columns, led by the brave Ney, pouring steadily forward straight for our ridge.

The firing became general as we opened on the advance; men had to shout to be audible to their neighbours; long lanes were ploughed through Picton's Division, and the balls went tearing through our cavalry in reserve, many of them striking the hospital farm, and some even travelling into the village beyond.

Bylandt's Dutch Belgians, posted in front of the cross-road, forgot their gallantry at Quatre Bras, and bolted, almost running over the Grenadiers of our 28th, who were restrained with difficulty from firing into them. One ball cut a tall tree into half at the hedgerow above the sandpit, bringing the feathery top down and half-smothering two doctors of the 95th, who had stationed themselves beneath it.

Nearly 24,000 men advanced, with loud cries and the hoarse rolling of drums, in four masses: Durutte against Papelotte, Alix and Marcognet in front of Kempt and Pack, Donzelot upon the devoted Rifles in La Haye Sainte, the shock taking place about two o'clock, and lasting for more than an hour.

Durutte took Papelotte, but was driven out again; Alix and Marcognet breasted the rise, and gained the ridge under a murderous discharge; the smell of trampled corn mingling with the powder smoke as the Great Battery ceased firing lest it should kill its comrades, and with shouts of *"Vive l'Empereur!"* the two columns hurled themselves against the steel barrier of bayonets on the hedge-lined bank above them.

Hand to hand, no quarter asked or given, veteran and conscript came on yelling like mad, Picton's Division meeting them in line.

Some of Marcognet's fellows crossed the Wavre road and blazed into the 92nd; but our men advanced, after a withering volley, and, jumping into the cross-road, went at them with a will. Cameron Highlanders, 32nd and 28th, Scots Royals, and Black Watch, Gordons and 44th, with colours waving and courage high, over the causeway they rushed, into the wheat and barley.

"Charge, charge! Hurrah!" cried Picton, his little black eyes sparkling, his florid complexion redder with excitement—a ball struck his right temple, he fell dead from his horse, and his men passed over him driving the foe down hill.

A mounted French officer had his horse shot, and getting

to his feet seized the regimental colour of the 32nd, which was nearly new. Belcher, who carried it, grasped the silk and the Frenchman groped for his sabre hilt, but Colour-sergeant Switzer thrust a pike at his breast. "Save the brave fellow!" was the cry, but it came too late; a private, named Lacy, fired point blank into him, and he fell lifeless.

Ney stood in the road beyond La Haye Sainte watching Donzelot's attack on the farm, where the "Green Germans" were forced, after a struggle, out of the long orchard into the buildings, and simultaneously a mass of Cuirassiers tore past the Hougoumont side and rode at the ridge.

Our Household Cavalry and Ponsonby's Heavies had walked on foot to the height overlooking the struggle; the trumpets rang out "Mount," and swinging into their saddles they swooped down into the thick of it. With a clatter across the causeway, and the muffled thunder of hoofs on the ground beyond it, the scarlet-coated Life Guards, wearing no armour then, and mounted on black horses, dashed past the Wellington tree into the potato field, with the Blues and King's Dragoon Guards, swinging, slashing, stirrup to stirrup, to meet Kellermann's troopers and Ordoner's Cuirassiers. There was the snort of eager horses, the creaking of leather, the clash of sword on steel cuirass, the yell of passion and the scream of agony; a seething mass of fighting-men and steeds, glinting and gleaming, swaying this way and that way, but always onward, jostling down the hill.

The 1st Lifes got jammed in the road beyond the farm with a body of Cuirassiers, on the spot where Ney had just before been standing, *voltigeurs* firing into them, on friend and foe alike!

Their Colonel, Ferrier, led eleven charges, although badly wounded by sabre and lance.

The King's Dragoons jumped their horses over a barrier of trees which our Rifles had built across the causeway and went thundering along that way, while the Blues were reaping a harvest of glory in another direction, and the 2nd Life Guards charged to the left for a great distance beyond the sandpit alongside the farm, where Corporal Shaw met his fate after slaying nine of the enemy single-handed.

After the battle men remembered this mighty swordsman, and told in solemn voices his deeds of derring-do. One cuirassier sat, out of the mêlée coolly loading his carbine and picking off our troopers, and it is believed he gave Shaw his mortal hurt.

A survivor narrated how, exhausted at nightfall, he had lain down on a dung-heap, when Shaw crawled beside him, bleeding from many wounds. In the morning the life-guardsman was still there, his head resting on his arm as if asleep, but it was the sleep which knows no waking.

Ponsonby's Union Brigade was meanwhile making its immortal onslaught, more towards Papelotte, the ground they went over being billowy, and the troops before them infantry of the line.

The Royals gave a ringing cheer; "Scotland for ever!" was the war-cry of the Greys; and the Inniskillings went in with an Irish howl.

As they passed the 92nd, many of the Highlanders caught hold of their stirrup-leathers and charged down with them; the very ground seemed trembling under the iron hoofs; Marcognet and Alix were broken and trampled, and in three minutes more than 2,000 prisoners were wending their disconsolate way to the rear.

"Those beautiful grey horses!" said Napoleon, as he watched the charge.

Did he see that struggle round the Eagle of his 45th, I wonder—that famous "Battle for the Standard" which Ansdell has painted so well?

What says Sergeant Ewart, the hero of the incident? "It

was in the charge I took the Eagle from the enemy. He and I had a hard contest for it. He made a thrust at my groin; I parried it off, and cut him down through the head. After this a lancer came at me; I threw the lance off by my right side, and cut him through the chin and upwards through the teeth, Next a foot-soldier fired at me, and then charged me with his bayonet, which I also had the good luck to parry, and then I cut him down through the head. Thus ended the contest."

Captain Clarke and Corporal Styles, of the Royals, took an Eagle from the 105th between them—a glorious gilded thing, embroidered with the names of Jéna, Eylau, Eckmühl, Essling, and Wagram—the gallant captain losing the tip of his nose in the struggle.

A man of the Inniskillings named Penfold claimed to have taken that colour; but his story is vague, and I incline to think that a blue silk camp-colour of the 105th, now at Abbotsford, was the one that Penfold seized and afterwards lost in the fray.

Sir William Ponsonby led the charge on a restive bay hack, and was killed; while some of the Greys got as far as the Great Battery, disabling many of the guns, and getting slain in the end.

Part of the 28th lost its head, and charged with the brigade; Lieutenant Deares of that regiment being taken prisoner, stripped of his clothes, rejoining at night in nothing but shirt and trousers.

Tathwell, of the Blues, tore off a colour, but his horse was shot and he lost it; and the greater part of the two brigades rode along the battery until heavy bodies of Cuirassiers and Lancers came to drive them back.

Vandeleur charged to their relief with his Light Dragoons—the 12th with bright yellow lancer facings, the 16th with scarlet, the buff 11th remaining in reserve.

"Squadrons, right half-wheel! Charge!" and the sabres of our light horsemen were soon busy in the valley below. The ground was very soft, for a month after the battle some of the holes made by horses' feet were measured, and found to be eighteen inches deep, and in speaking of artillery movements it must be remembered that the guns were at times up to the axle in clay.

The heavy cavalry regained our position; but so much had they suffered that, later in the day, when they were drawn up in line to show a bold front, there were only fifty of them; Somerset, who led the "Households," losing his hat, and wearing the helmet of a life-guardsman, with its red and blue worsted crest, until nightfall.

The attack had failed, and there was a long pause, broken only by the firing at Hougoumont and some feeble attempts on La Haye Sainte; but it was now the turn of our troops in the centre, from the *chaussée* to the back of the *château*; and a terrible time they had!

A renewal of the cannonade—a forming of our regiments into squares and oblongs—and then the grandest cavalry affair in history, as forty squadrons of Cuirassiers and Dragoons crossed from the French right in beautiful order, wheeled up until they almost filled the space from Hougoumont to La Haye Sainte, and, about four o'clock, put spurs to their horses and began the Third Attack!

A forest of sword-blades, an undulating sea of helmets, a roar of mighty shouting as they came through the yet untrampled grain.

Wave after wave, far as the eye could scan, now glinting with thousands of bright points as the sullen sun shone for a moment upon them, now grey and sombre as the clouds closed together again. Nearer! nearer! nearer! Men clutched their muskets tighter and breathed hard; gunners rammed home and hastened to re-load before the smoke had drifted from the cannon.

Suddenly they left their guns, and ran to the infantry for protection as the sea burst upon us, and our ridge became alive with furious horsemen, surging and foaming round and round the squares. There were many who thought that all was over, but the little clumps of scarlet fringed with steel were impenetrable.

In vain the moustached troopers cut desperately at the bayonets; in vain they rode up and fired their pistols into the faces of our lads. For three-quarters of an hour they expended their strength in a hopeless task; and when our fresh cavalry from Dörnberg's and Grant's Brigades charged them, they went down the slope again, leaving the ground dotted with dead and dying.

A moment's respite to re-form in the hollows below, and back they came once more, in the face of a fearful fire from our artillery, whose guns were double-shotted—some loaded with scattering grape and canister. Lanes, sickening to behold, were torn through the squadrons; but Milhaud's men were not to be daunted, and the same strange scene was repeated many times.

A small body of cuirassiers that had surrendered was being escorted to the rear by a weak party of the 7th Hussars, when they made a bold dash for liberty along the Nivelle road, stampeding, *ventre à terre*, until they reached the abattis at the end of the Hougoumont avenue.

Here they met Ross's company of the 51st, who killed eight men and twelve horses, the rest—about sixty—surrendering again.

One artilleryman was seen under his gun, dodging a French trooper, who tried to reach him with his long sword.

After some moments the cuirassier's horse was shot, and the gunner, sallying out, hit him over the head with his rammer, and packed him and off to the rear with a parting kick.

The ridge was once more cleared, and Mercer's battery brought into the front line. The whole field was now littered with corpses and accoutrements. Gaily-dressed trumpeters, and officers on whose breasts hung crosses of the Legion of

Honour, lay bleeding in the barley among hundreds of dead and wounded horses. Here a lancer in green and light blue, there a heap of cuirassiers of the 1st Regiment, mown down by grape shot; yonder a *chasseur-à-cheval*, propped against his charger, while swords and cuirasses were almost as numerous as the stalks of corn.

All the slope was torn and trampled; flies were busy in the now loathsome hollows; there was constant firing still at Hougoumont and La Haye Sainte, when the trumpets sounded again, seventy-seven squadrons, including the cavalry of the Guard, France returned to the charge. Every arm of the mounted service was represented in this attack, the beauty and brilliancy of the uniforms baffling description. Carabiniers, white-coated, with brass cuirasses and red crested helmets; Lancers, Dragoons, and Chasseurs in green, with facings of every hue; the Red Lancers of the Guard, clad in scarlet from head to heel, and Napoleon's own favourite *chasseurs-à-cheval*, with hussar caps and red pelisses, richly braided with orange lace; tall bear-skinned Horse Grenadiers, with white facings to their blue coats; the Cuirassiers, dark and sombre looking; the high felt shakoes of the Hussars—it was as though a flower garden in all its summer dress were moving at a slow trot upon us, heralded by the thunder of hell from the batteries behind it.

When the thunder stopped, which it always did as the leading files reached the crest of the ridge, our men could hear in the momentary intervals of their own firing the jingling of bits and scabbards, and the heavy breathing of the horses. Mounted skirmishers came close to the batteries and commenced firing at the gunners, who were literally dripping with perspiration from the exertions they made. One fellow took several pot-shots at Captain Mercer, who was coolly walking his horse backwards and forwards along a bank to set an example to his men. He missed each time, and grinned grimly as he reloaded, but as the head of the squadrons closed up the skirmishers vanished and were succeeded by the rush which threatened death to every soul on the plateau. Wellington's orders were to retire into the squares and leave the batteries, but Mercer's men stuck to their guns, repulsing three charges of the Horse Grenadiers and dealing such slaughter that the position of "G Troop" was known next day by the enormous heap of slain lying before it, visible from a considerable distance.

The carnage on the slope was shocking—the oldest soldiers had seen nothing like it men and horses lay piled one on another, five and six in a heap, every fresh discharge adding to the ghastly pyramid. The 1st Cuirassiers numbered 300 of the Legion of Honour in its ranks—it lost 117, including two lieutenants and the brave Captain Poinsot, page to the Emperor in 1807, wounded at Moscow and Brienne. One officer, finding the fire from a particular gun playing havoc with his men, rode straight at it and was blown to atoms.

The horses during the battle suffered cruelly, and some of the details are heartrending the charger of a very stout officer with the Duke's staff, probably Müffling, was seen to rear for some time without the rider being able to bring it down—its front legs had been both shot off. Another trooper's horse was seen next morning sitting on its tail, its hind legs gone; and one poor beast ran for sympathy to six guns in succession, and was driven off from each with exclamations of horror until it reached "G Troop," where they mercifully killed it: the whole of its face below the great brown pleading eyes had been carried away by a round shot!

After a repulse and a re-attack, the remnant of the seventy-seven squadrons reeled back to their own lines the cavalry of France, magnificent, irresistible, brave as lions, and nobly led, had shattered itself without result, and the third great attempt had failed!

All the afternoon there had been great doings at Hougoumont. About one o'clock Colonel Hepburn had relieved Saltoun in the large orchard with a battalion of the 3rd—now the
Scots Guards—and the combat on that side became a long
succession of advances with the bayonet to the front hedge
and retirings into a green dry ditch, which is known to us as
the "friendly hollow-way." When our men fell back, a terrific
fire from the short east wall would stagger the foe, and the
Scots, having formed again, would scramble out of the hollow
and clear the orchard of all but the dead.

Along the terrible south wall a staff-officer, who had been
through all the Peninsula battles, afterwards said that the slain
lay thicker than he had ever seen them elsewhere.

The *château* and barns were now burning furiously, fired
by Haxo's howitzers at Napoleon's orders, and many of our
wounded perished in the flames; some officers' horses tore
out of the barn, galloped madly round the yard, and rushed
into the fire again to be destroyed.

Twice the enemy got in: once by a little door in the west
wall, through which they never got out alive; and the second
time, when our Guardsmen had sallied out into the lane to
drive off a body of infantry, about fifty French entered on
their heels through the north gate. Then, by main strength of
arm, Colonel Macdonell, Sergeant Graham, and three or four
more, shut and barred the wooden gate in the faces of the
others, and those inside were all shot down.

A brave fellow climbed on to the beam that crossed the
gateway; but Graham fired, and he dropped with a scream on
to the heads of his comrades outside the wall.

The fire stopped at the door of the château chapel, which
was full of wounded, and a wooden figure of our Saviour
had the feet nibbled by the flames, at which the superstitious
marvel greatly to this day.

Columns of smoke hung over everything. A gallant artillery driver rushed his horses to the wall, and flung a barrel of welcome cartridges over into the yard. At the corner, before the gardener's house, Baron de Cubières lay wounded under his horse; afterwards, when Governor of Ancona, he expressed himself very grateful that we had not fired on him!

Crawford of the 3rd Guards was killed in the kitchen garden, Blackman of the Coldstreams died in the orchard; but the attack and repulse grew gradually weaker, as both sides tired of the hideous slaughter.

Meanwhile, a serious trouble which had been menacing the Emperor on his right flank for some time at last grew terribly imminent.

The Prussians were coming in spite of Grouchy, who had been sent in their pursuit.

They should have arrived about one o'clock; but, thanks to the bad roads, a fire in the town of Wavre, which had to be extinguished before the ammunition-wagons could be got through, and some hesitation on the part of Gneisenau, Blücher's Chief of Staff, who doubted Wellington's good faith, it was half-past four when part of Bülow's corps came out of the woods at St. Lambert and confirmed Napoleon's previously awakened fears.

In the hazy weather they thought it was Grouchy, and a false report was afterwards sent through the French army to cheer the wearied men; but the Emperor and Soult knew otherwise, and the line of battle was weakened by a strong force being detached to meet the new arrivals.

There was no time to be lost; drums rolled and trumpets sounded again, and the last remnants of the cavalry had not regained their position when the Fourth Grand Attack began with a fury that even exceeded the others.

While fresh bodies of horse and foot advanced up the ridge, a most determined rush was made on La Haye Sainte. Baring had been reinforced, it is true; but, although he sent time after time for more ammunition, not a single cartridge was forthcoming!

A feeble excuse has been made that there were no means of getting it into the building; but a large door and several windows faced our line at the back of the house then, as now. They may still be seen by the visitor to Waterloo.

A horde of French infantry flung themselves on the buildings, setting the barn on fire, and besieging the broken gateway.

While the brave Germans filled their camp-kettles from the pond and extinguished the flames, others, with their bayonets only, kept the door leading into the field. Seventeen corpses they piled up there in a few minutes, one gallant fellow defending a breach with a brick torn from the wall! The individual acts of heroism on authentic record would fill many pages but, without ammunition, they were at a fearful disadvantage.

The *voltigeurs* climbed on to the roof of the stable, and shot them down at their ease: the half barn-door is preserved to the present day, with eighty bullet-holes in it! Alten sent the brave Christian Ompteda to their aid, if practicable, with the 5th Battalion. He pointed to an overwhelming force; but the irrepressible Orange repeated Alten's suggestion in a tone that brooked no delay, and Ompteda went down with his 5th Battalion, and they died, almost to a man!

Baring dismounted to pick up his cap, knocked off by a shot; four balls had lodged in the cloak rolled on his saddle-bow, and a fifth then pierced the saddle itself, while the Scotch Lieutenant Græme, sitting on the rafters of the piggery, in which a calf was lowing, raised his shako to cheer his men, and his right hand was taken off at the wrist. He was only eighteen.

It was hopeless. "If I receive no cartridges," said Baring in his last appeal, "I not only must, but will abandon the post!" And very soon those neglected heroes retreated slowly through the house and out through the garden beyond, the French, bursting into the yard, chasing, the remnant round and round and bayoneting them on the dung-heaps.

A roar of cheering rang above the battle. At last they were victorious, and the French had taken La Haye Sainte.

Without a moment's hesitation their conquest was turned to the best possible advantage. Smart red-braided Horse Artillery galloped down the causeway, dragging their guns to the knoll above the sandpit, from which our 95th had been driven, and, unlimbering, opened fire at sixty yards range on to our line.

Skirmishers filled the hedgerows and the farm buildings. The Great Battery renewed its work of death, and in a few moments there was a serious gap in the centre of our position.

Lambert's brigade had been brought up before this, and suffered terribly.

The 27th, which had lain down and slept soundly behind Mont St. Jean until after three o'clock, lost 478 out of 698 in its new quarters; and the 40th thirteen officers and 180 rank and file, one round shot taking off the head of Captain Fisher and killing twenty-five men.

Ompteda's brigade mustered a mere handful, Kielmansegge was almost destroyed, Halkett had two weak squares, one of his regiments being very shaky indeed, and, altogether, things were unpleasant when the Duke came up with reinforcements to patch our front as best he could.

Far off on our right Chassé's Dutch Belgians had arrived, shouting and singing, from Braine l'Alleud, very drunk, narrowly escaping a volley from us, as they wore the French uniform; and at this time, by reason of the bolting of Hake's Cumberland Hussars and some of our supports, with the enormous losses from the six hours of carnage, the British affairs were in bad case.

Halkett's 30th and 73rd in square had been charged no less than eleven times: the Duke pointed to a scarlet mass in front through the smoke, and inquired what regiment it was. It was the dead and wounded of those two corps, huddled together where they had fallen.

The green-faced 73rd was at one time commanded by Lieutenant Stewart, all the other officers having been killed or wounded; and at half-past seven the colours of both regiments were sent to the rear.

The 2nd Line Battalion of the German Legion went into action with 300 men, but mustered only six officers and thirty-six privates after the battle; but Blücher was now nearing the French right rear with nearly 52,000 troops and 104 guns, and the Emperor was obliged to send General Duhesme with eight battalions of the young Guard down into the straggling village of Planchenoit to help to check them.

He had been at La Belle Alliance all day, and Prussian shot were now falling about him.

Marshal Ney sent for more infantry to renew the attack. *"Où voulez vous que j'en prenne: voulez vous que j'en fasse?"* was the Emperor's impatient reply—"Where can I get them: do you wish me to make them?"

The long June day was drawing into evening, and shadows began to lengthen across the fields. Wellington, who had always been seen where the fire was hottest, rode with a calm, inscrutable face, followed by a sadly diminished staff, his eagle eye taking note of the strength and weakness of our line.

The Hussars had been moved in rear of the centre; and Adams' Brigade took position immediately behind the ridge. In front of the clover field where the 52nd stood in square, a pretty little tortoiseshell kitten, which had been frightened out of Hougoumont by the firing, lay dead—a strange feature in the scene of destruction.

The men were growing accustomed to the hideous sights

and sounds around them, and became impatient at the inactivity which doomed them to endure without reprisal. Suddenly the brass guns blazed forth once more upon us; the pas de charge was rolling from a thousand drums; a serried line was seen advancing along our entire front, and, led by the Emperor himself, on his grey charger Marie, his famous *redingote gris* open and showing the well-known dark-green chasseur coat, the Grenadiers of the Guard marched in solid columns into the valley.

Two winding serpents of determined men ten battalions in tall black bearskins, white facings and dark-blue pantaloons—that was their dress at Waterloo—with Friant and Morand, Petit, whom Napoleon had kissed at Fontainebleau, Poret de Morvan, and old Cambronne. The *élite* of the French army, the Grenadiers and Chasseurs of the Old and Middle Guard, marching sternly to victory or death. Marcognet, Alix, and Donzelot, with their remnants, against our reeling left; Reille, Foy, and Jérôme renewing on Hougoumont—cavalry in the gaps and spaces—a simultaneous, mighty Last Attack!

The yet unbroken Imperial Guard set their faces towards the spot where Maitland's, Adams' and Byng's red-coats looked to their priming and closed their ranks had Napoleon hurled them against the cross road behind La Haye Sainte, the story of Waterloo had been written differently.

He missed his chance; he threw away his final hope. The greatest of his many mistakes was committed, and, handing over the leadership to Ney, he remained on a hillock above the farm, and watched the downfall of France and the death-blow of his empire! For the last time in this world their Emperor addressed them, pointing towards the heights with a gesture all could understand.

"*Déployez les aigles. En avant! Vive l'Empereur!*" and with a great shout they quickened their pace, passing proudly, unheeding, over the bodies of those comrades who had gone before.

Red tongues of flame burst from the smoke of our guns; whiz, came the fiery rockets, darting into their ranks, scorching, blinding, and burning in their course; humming shells dropped among them with terrible destruction; but the Old Guard pressed on, and began to mount the ridge.

Ney's horse fell—the fifth killed under him that day, and the "bravest of the brave," went forward on foot. Alas, would that it had been to death!

Our Guards were lying down to avoid the hurricane from the French artillery. A shell dropped in one of the squares, and Colonel Colquitt, picking it up, fizzing and fuming, walked to the edge and flung it outside to burst harmlessly. Another officer, mortally wounded, said faintly:

"I should like to see the colours of the regiment again before I quit them for ever": they were brought and waved round his body, and with a smile, he was carried away, to die.

It was men like those that the oncoming columns had to face, and batteries as famous as those of Bull and Bolton, of Norman Ramsay, Whinyates, and Webber Smith, with guns double shotted and served as on parade; no need to sight so carefully, for the moving target is a wide one, and they hit in every time!

Now the skirmishers run out, shouting and firing as before, and when they have said their say, they fall back leaving all clear for the others; but the columns seem to get no nearer though they are marching steadily; front rank after front rank is blown to shreds—that is why they appear stationary!

The gunners have done their work; the guns recoil, and are left there it is the turn of the infantry now, and the time has come, for that historic signal, "Up, Guards, and at 'em!" which in reality was never said.

But whatever the word was, they do "up," and they do "at 'em"; and again it is bayonet to bayonet, and man to man.

One Welsh giant, named Hughes, six feet seven inches in

height, is seen to knock over a dozen of the Old Guard single handed; the red-coats and the blue-coats mingle for a moment and the blue-coats melt away.

The second column, a little behind the other, is in good order it has suffered less from the cannonade, and is full of fire and fury; but so also are our 52nd lads, who advance down the slope with three tremendous cheers.

Colborne is leading, and when they get abreast of the column he cries–

"Halt! Mark time!"

The men touch in to their left, and regain their dressing; Colborne's horse is shot, and he comes forward wiping his mouth with a white handkerchief, still wearing Ensign Leeke's blue boat-cloak.

"Right shoulders forward!"

The regiment swings round, and, four deep, faces the column's flank two hundred yards away.

"Forward, 52nd—charge!" and the Foot Guards, who are back on the ridge again, behold a noble spectacle.

The crash is terrific; the Imperial phalanx is taken in flank. The contest is fierce, but it is soon over.

Brave Michel, in response to our officers, replies with glorious esprit de corps, "The Guard dies, and never surrenders!" his words instantly fulfilled, as he falls lifeless, sword in hand, while Cambronne, grown old in the service (to whom these words have been falsely attributed), gives up his weapon to William Halkett.

Halkett's horse is shot, and Cambronne hastens away, but his captor is too quick for him, and seizing his gold aiguillette, hands him to a sergeant to be taken care of.

On presses the 52nd, driving the broken Guard before it: it is a sight probably never repeated in history—one regiment traversing the field alone, in sight of the army sending the foe like sheep into the hollow dispersing and pushing them relentlessly back, until they turn and fly, and other corps make haste to join in that glorious progress.

There is a movement along the ridge as the setting sun shines out in a burst of sinking splendour, and the Duke, with cocked hat raised above his head, gives the magic word, "The whole line will advance!" and then spurs down after the 52nd.

On the rising ground near La Haye Sainte, Napoleon sits on horseback, close to a small battalion which has formed square.

Jérôme, his brother, bleeding and exhausted, is with him, with honest old Drouot in his artillery uniform, in the pocket of which is a well-worn Bible; Soult and Gourgaud, Bertrand and brave young La Bédoyère are there, too: but the English Hussars are coming on at a fast trot.

All day long the waves of valour have been rolling northward, and breaking against an ironbound shore; now the tide has turned, and rushes madly south again.

Nothing but confusion meets the eye: everywhere the French are in full retreat—solitary men, groups of three and four, ruined regiments, and the skeletons of squadrons.

Jérôme rides close to his brother, and says in a meaning tone—

"It were well for all who bear the name of Bonaparte to perish here!"

Napoleon orders some guns to open on the Hussars, and one shot hits Lord Uxbridge on the right knee as, mounted on a troop horse belonging to a sergeant-major of the 23rd Light Dragoons, he is leading the pursuit.

"Here we must die on the field of battle," exclaims the Emperor, preparing to head the weak column; but Soult seizes his bridle, saying, "They will not kill you, you will be taken prisoner"; and, held up in the saddle by two faithful officers, for he is worn out, Napoleon is galloped away in the gathering darkness.

On the left of the Brussels road some Prussian guns had come up and fired on our men.

They were the sole representatives of Blücher's force present before Mont St. Jean until after the retreat had begun; and they had been far better absent, as their pounding was cruelly felt by Mercer's battery and several of our regiments.

They were induced, after some time, to change the direction of their range, and then all went well. The 52nd still pursued its march, halting for a moment near La Haye Sainte to face and charge some rallying squares, where a Belgian soldier was seen killing a wounded Frenchman, and was run through by an officer of the regiment.

Leeke, who carried the King's colour, found a foot and a half of the pole wet with blood; Holman, the brother of the blind traveller, had three musket balls through his sword blade, and wore it for many years; Colborne and Major Rowan, being both dismounted, jumped on to two horses attached to an abandoned gun, calling to their men to cut the harness; but the advance continuing, they had to dismount with a hearty laugh and march on again on foot.

It was getting dark, and our Hussars were clearing the field in splendid style, the 10th, whose sabres were soon red as their scarlet cuffs, engaging with some strong remnants of the Old Guard and losing two officers.

Major Murray, of the dashing 18th, met a gun going at full speed, and leaped his charger over the traces, between the leaders and wheelers, while his men proceeded to cut the gunners down.

Colquhoun Grant, who had lost five horses and was then mounted on a magnificent chestnut, sent the gallant remains of his brigade at the retreating foe; and until it was impossible any longer to pick one's way among the vast heaps of dead, disabled cannon, and miserable wounded—in short, the absolute wreck of an army—our light cavalry went wheeling and slashing right and left, hurrying on the veteran, the conscript, the artillery driver and the officer alike, all the French accounts doing justice to these light horsemen. It is only in private letters, hardly, in the official documents, that England can learn the heroism of her Hussars at Waterloo.

Meanwhile the 52nd had crossed to the left of the road and scattered a column debouching from Planchenoit, behind the buildings of La Belle Alliance, in front of which a mass of guns had been left to their fate. The regiment passed on, and on its return found them marked with the numbers of other corps that had succeeded them.

All the causeway was crammed with flying troops a terrible struggle for liberty took place, in which discipline gave way to terror. General officer and baggage wagon fled side by side; rifles and accoutrements were thrown away that their owners might hurry faster. The fields, the by-lanes, the woods, were all filled with fugitives—even the Emperor had to turn aside in order to get past.

Marshal Ney was one of the last to go. He had joined the army on the 15th, without money, without horses, almost without a uniform. He was to be found everywhere on that dreadful 18th, planting batteries, heading charges, rallying, raging, facing death at every stride, and when it was over he tottered exhausted away on foot, leaning on the shoulder of a compassionate corporal.

Now the Prussians have arrived in force. Planchenoit, its churchyard and crooked street, its orchards and barnyards, are full of French and Prussian slain.

The young Guard fought well, but they were outnumbered, and Blücher rides into the *chaussée* at La Belle Alliance.

A Uhlan band plays "God Save the King," and farther along the road they meet the Duke returning on his way in the dark to write his despatches announcing the victory.

The two soldiers embrace, and sit talking for ten minutes while the stream goes hurrying by. Then the fiery old German follows the retreat with a fury that is incredible.

At Genappe the Silesians have taken the Emperor's baggage; Gneisenau mounts a drummer on one of the cream-coloured carriage horses, and away they go into the darkness after the fugitives, driving them from seven bivouacs, slaying, hacking, giving no rest, until the land is strewn for leagues with dead men, fallen under the Prussian steel.

Merciless it may seem to us, looking back with fourscore years between us and that moonlit night; but such was the vitality of the French that the most drastic steps were necessary to prevent their army mustering again.

What can I say of the battle-field, after the pursuit had rolled away, and it was left to the searcher and the plunderer?

If I could re-create one tithe of the horror those slopes and roads revealed you would sicken and turn away in disgust.

Prussian, Belgian, and British, there were, out on the plain that night, bent on no errand of mercy; stragglers and camp-followers creeping from group to group, tearing the rings from the fingers, and the teeth from the jaws!

Many a life was foully taken that tender nursing might have saved; but there were some groups who sought for a lost comrade or a favourite officer, and women there were, with woman's gentle sympathy, soothing and tending as only they can soothe.

The bulk of the British force had gone to bivouac beyond and about Rosomme, which was behind the French position; but some detached portions remained where they had fought, too weary to advance with the others.

Mercer was one of these, and creeping under the cover of a wagon, worn out with slaughter, he slept—waking to find a dead man stark and stiff beneath him! His men came to him in the morning, and asked permission to bury one of their comrades.

"Why him in particular?" asked the captain, for many a bearskin-crested helmet was empty in "G Troop."

Then they showed him the horror of it.

The whole of the man's head had been carried away, leaving the fleshy mask of what had been a face, from which the eyes were still staring wildly.

"We have not slept a wink, sir," they said. "Those eyes have haunted us all night!"

With daybreak men stood aghast at the spectacle of that battle-ground.

The losses have never been satisfactorily reckoned; but I have seen it stated, curiously, that of the red-coats 9,999 were actually killed there. The French loss for the four days campaign has been counted as 50,000.

Every house in the neighbourhood was full of wounded. For three days, the doctors tell us, they were being brought in by the search parties, a sharp frost having congealed the wounds of many and so saved them, and lines of carts jolted the shrieking wretches over that dreadful causeway to Brussels in endless succession.

At Hougoumont, where the orange-trees were in blossom, they flung three hundred bodies down a well: it was a simple method, saving time and trouble; but a dark tradition lingers that voices were heard afterwards, faintly imploring, from the cavernous depths.

Wild strawberries hung their red clusters, and the little, blue forget-me-not peeped in the woods; birds of prey came croaking on the wing; and within twenty-four hours ten thousand horses had been flayed by the Flemish peasants, many of whom made fortunes by plunder! Men gathered jewelled decorations and crosses by handfuls it was impossible to take three strides without treading on a sword, a broken musket, a carbine, or a corpse!

Near La Haye Sainte they found a pretty French girl in hussar uniform, and the farm itself was encrusted with blood; tufts of hair adhered to the doorways, the yard presenting a sight never to be forgotten. A pole to which a scrap of torn silk clung was picked up under the body of Ensign Nettles: it was the King's colour.

The remains of three French brothers named Angelet were among the slain, and the history of one was most romantic. Wounded in some of the Napoleonic wars, where he had lost a leg, he was taunted by a lady with the fact that he could only talk of what he had done for France—that he could do no more. The brave fellow seized his crutches, limped after the army, and met his fate at Waterloo.

Picton's body—wounded at Quatre Bras, though none but his valet knew it—was taken to England, and by a strange coincidence was laid, at the Fountain Inn, Canterbury, on the very table at which he had dined, a fortnight before, on his way to join the army.

Byng of the Guards said to Sir John Colborne in Paris: "How do your fellows like our getting the credit of what you did at Waterloo? I could not advance because our ammunition was all done."

The Foot Guards got their bearskins as a well-merited reward, only the Grenadier companies wearing them during the battle. The 52nd, for their great share in the closing scene, received—nothing! and the Duke, when approached on the subject of that glaring injustice, said, "Oh, I know nothing of the services of particular regiments. There was glory enough for all!"

LEONAUR

ALSO FROM LEONAUR
AVAILABLE IN SOFTCOVER OR HARDCOVER WITH DUST JACKET

SEPOYS, SIEGE & STORM *by Charles John Griffiths*—The Experiences of a young officer of H.M.'s 61st Regiment at Ferozepore, Delhi ridge and at the fall of Delhi during the Indian mutiny 1857.

CAMPAIGNING IN ZULULAND *by W. E. Montague*—Experiences on campaign during the Zulu war of 1879 with the 94th Regiment.

THE STORY OF THE GUIDES *by G. J. Younghusband*—The Exploits of the Soldiers of the famous Indian Army Regiment from the northwest frontier 1847 - 1900..

ZULU: 1879 *by D.C.F. Moodie & the Leonaur Editors*—The Anglo-Zulu War of 1879 from contemporary sources: First Hand Accounts, Interviews, Dispatches, Official Documents & Newspaper Reports.

THE RECOLLECTIONS OF SKINNER OF SKINNER'S HORSE *by James Skinner*—James Skinner and his 'Yellow Boys' Irregular cavalry in the wars of India between the British, Mahratta, Rajput, Mogul, Sikh & Pindarree Forces.

TOMMY ATKINS' WAR STORIES 14 FIRST HAND ACCOUNTS—Fourteen first hand accounts from the ranks of the British Army during Queen Victoria's Empire Original & True Battle Stories Recollections of the Indian Mutiny With the 49th in the Crimea With the Guards in Egypt The Charge of the Six Hundred With Wolseley in Ashanti Alma, Inkermann and Magdala With the Gunners at Tel-el-Kebir Russian Guns and Indian Rebels Rough Work in the Crimea In the Maori Rising Facing the Zulus From Sebastopol to Lucknow Sent to Save Gordon On the March to Chitral Tommy by Rudyard Kipling

CHASSEUR OF 1914 *by Marcel Dupont*—Experiences of the twilight of the French Light Cavalry by a young officer during the early battles of the great war in Europe.

TROOP HORSE & TRENCH *by R. A. Lloyd*—The experiences of a British Lifeguardsman of the household cavalry fighting on the western front during the First World War 1914-18.

THE EAST AFRICAN MOUNTED RIFLES *by C. J. Wilson*—Experiences of the campaign in the East African bush during the First World War.

THE FIGHTING CAMELIERS *by Frank Reid*—The exploits of the Imperial Camel Corps in the desert and Palestine campaigns of the First World War.

LEONAUR

ALSO FROM LEONAUR

AVAILABLE IN SOFTCOVER OR HARDCOVER WITH DUST JACKET

THE COMPLEAT RIFLEMAN HARRIS *by Benjamin Harris as told to & transcribed by Captain Henry Curling*—The adventures of a soldier of the 95th (Rifles) during the Peninsular Campaign of the Napoleonic Wars

WITH WELLINGTON'S LIGHT CAVALRY *by William Tomkinson*—The Experiences of an officer of the 16th Light Dragoons in the Peninsular and Waterloo campaigns of the Napoleonic Wars.

SERGEANT BOURGOGNE *by Adrien Bourgogne*—With Napoleon's Imperial Guard in the Russian Campaign and on the Retreat from Moscow 1812 - 13.

SWORDS OF HONOUR *by Henry Newbolt & Stanley L. Wood*—The Careers of Six Outstanding Officers from the Napoleonic Wars, the Wars for India and the American Civil War, with dozens of illustrations by Stanley L. Wood.

SURTEES OF THE RIFLES *by William Surtees*—A Soldier of the 95th (Rifles) in the Peninsular campaign of the Napoleonic Wars.

ENSIGN BELL IN THE PENINSULAR WAR *by George Bell*—The Experiences of a young British Soldier of the 34th Regiment 'The Cumberland Gentlemen' in the Napoleonic wars.

HUSSAR IN WINTER *by Alexander Gordon*—A British Cavalry Officer during the retreat to Corunna in the Peninsular campaign of the Napoleonic Wars.

NAPOLEONIC WAR STORIES *by Sir Arthur Quiller-Couch*—Tales of soldiers, spies, battles & sieges from the Peninsular & Waterloo campaigns.

JOURNALS OF ROBERT ROGERS OF THE RANGERS *by Robert Rogers*—The exploits of Rogers & the Rangers in his own words during 1755-1761 in the French & Indian War.

KERSHAW'S BRIGADE VOLUME 1 *by D. Augustus Dickert*—Manassas, Seven Pines, Sharpsburg (Antietam), Fredricksburg, Chancellorsville, Gettysburg, Chickamauga, Chattanooga, Fort Sanders & Bean Station..

KERSHAW'S BRIGADE VOLUME 2 *by D. Augustus Dickert*—At the wilderness, Cold Harbour, Petersburg, The Shenandoah Valley and Cedar Creek.

A TIGER ON HORSEBACK *by L. March Phillips*—The Experiences of a Trooper & Officer of Rimington's Guides - The Tigers - during the Anglo-Boer war 1899 - 1902.

Printed in the United Kingdom
by Lightning Source UK Ltd.
126267UK00001B/285/A

9 781846 772405